a touch of tropical
spice

From Chili Crab to Laksa

75 Fabulous Recipes from Monsoon Asia

Recipes from
Four Seasons Hotels and Resorts

Foreword by Nobu

Introduction by Wendy Hutton

Photography by Masano Kawana

Styling by Christina Ong

TUTTLE PUBLISHING
Tokyo • Rutland, Vermont • Singapore

Published by Tuttle Publishing, an imprint of Periplus Editions (HK) Ltd., with editorial offices at 364 Innovation Drive, North Clarendon, Vermont 05759 USA and 61 Tai Seng Avenue, #02-12, Singapore 534167

ISBN-13: 978-0-8048-4081-1
(previously published as Tropical Asian Cooking)

Distributed by
North America, Latin America & Europe
Tuttle Publishing,364 Innovation Drive
North Clarendon, VT 05759-9436 U.S.A.
Tel: 1 (802) 773-8930; Fax: 1 (802) 773-6993
info@tuttlepublishing.com
www.tuttlepublishing.com

Japan
Tuttle Publishing, Yaekari Building, 3rd Floor
5-4-12 Osaki, Shinagawa-ku
Tokyo 141 0032
Tel: (81) 03 5437-0171; Fax: (81) 03 5437-0755
tuttle-sales@gol.com

Asia Pacific
Berkeley Books Pte. Ltd.
61 Tai Seng Avenue, #02-12, Singapore 534167
Tel: (65) 6280-1330; Fax: (65) 6280-6290
inquiries@periplus.com.sg
www.periplus.com

Indonesia
PT Java Books Indonesia
Kawasan Industri Pulogadung, Jl. Rawa Gelam IV No. 9
Jakarta 13930
Tel: (62) 21 4682-1088, Fax: (62) 21 461-0206
cs@javabooks.co.id

12 11 10 09   5 4 3 2 1

Printed in Hong Kong

contents

foreword by nobu

This book truly represents the contemporary flavors of tropical South and Southeast Asia today. It is unashamedly Asian without being traditional—reflecting the fascinating blend of peoples and cultures found in the region. What is particularly fascinating to me is the interaction between the cuisines—the new combinations that arise, combining and yet preserving the distinctive character and strength of the indigenous dishes and ingredients.

This modern, fresh approach to Asian cooking is the kind of food I love—honest food that is easy to put together and guaranteed to please. I have been fortunate to cook at several of the Four Seasons hotels throughout Asia, swapping tips with chefs who hail from every corner of the region. Herewith are presented a selection of their best recipes that are absolutely perfect for every occasion—from a simple breakfast for two, to an alfresco picnic or barbecue, to an elegant dinner party with friends at home.

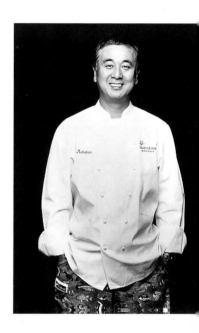

Nobuyuki Matsuhisa

dining in the tropics

Lands where soft tropical breezes carry a hint of spices and scented flowers, where warm seas bathe coral reefs teeming with fish, where life-giving monsoon rains nourish an endless variety of lush fruit, vegetables, and intensely aromatic herbs … who has not dreamed of tropical Asia, and longed to experience its sensuous beauty?

Fortunately, it's not essential to travel to enjoy the exquisite flavors of some of the world's most exciting and creative cuisines, encapsulating all that is magical in these exotic lands. Try any of the recipes within these pages and you're already halfway there.

For centuries, some of the most precious produce of the region has been sought by the West: pepper and cardamom from India, nutmeg and cloves from Indonesia's Spice Islands, cinnamon from Sri Lanka, and galangal root from mainland Southeast Asia. Today, there's a lot more than spices on supermarket shelves. Thanks to increased international travel, and to migration and the consequent opening of ethnic restaurants, Asian markets and specialty shops—the diverse flavors of tropical Asia can be recreated in kitchens around the world.

This collection of recipes includes the major cuisines of tropical Asia. While some classic dishes are included, many also incorporate a new approach to the region's cuisines. No longer confined by tradition or isolated by limited communications, Asian cooks are happily borrowing the cooking styles and ingredients of their neighbors, or from even further afield. Many traditional dishes have been modified for a fresher, lighter taste, adapted to suit today's health-conscious gourmets.

Luxurious hotels in tropical Asia—such as the highly esteemed Four Seasons properties—have been at the forefront of the evolution of the "new" tropical cuisine. Their chefs come from a wide range of backgrounds, and their sharing of knowledge and experience has led to exciting adapations and variations. A Balinese may work together with a Swiss who happens to have spent time in Tokyo to create new types of sushi; a Singaporean chef and his Thai colleague may jointly create a new twist to a classic laksa noodle soup; a Maldivian chef may discuss with his French counterpart how to improve a traditional vegetable curry, or decide to use olive oil rather than saturated coconut oil. In this collection of fabulous recipes, chefs of Four Seasons properties around the region share with us just such recipes which have been carefully adapted for use in the home kitchen.

The recipes featured in this book are inspired by the cuisines of tropical India; of the Indian Ocean archipelago of the Maldives; the islands of Indonesia and Singapore, and—on the Southeast Asian mainland—Malaysia, Thailand and Vietnam.

Tropical central and southern India have produced a style of cooking that has not only spread into nearby countries such as the Maldives, but which has traveled with Indian migrants as far as Singapore and Malaysia. Yet the influence has not been one way, for

centuries earlier, some of the spices of Indonesia's Moluccan islands—especially cloves, nutmeg, and mace—found their way into Indian spice chests.

Apart from the liberal use of spices, the food of India and the Maldives is often pungent with chilies, although their heat is frequently soothed by the rich coconut milk added to gravies and sauces. Yogurt, too, adds a cooling touch to sides, salads and drinks.

Tropical seasonings not found in cooler regions of India—including the inimitable curry leaves and pungent brown mustard seeds—add a distinctive note to many dishes. Borrowed from northern India, widely popular seasoning mixes or masala such as the spicy flavorings of tandoori food are quite happily incorporated into tropical-style grills.

Surrounded by the warm waters of the Indian Ocean, the inhabitants of the Maldives naturally enjoy fish as their major source of protein. This appears in many guises, such as fish and pineapple curry; grilled fish nuggets in spices; pan-fried flakey tuna cakes with a coconut green curry dip; and barbecued jumbo shrimp with chili dip.

The major cuisines of Southeast Asia—Thai, Vietnamese, Malaysian, Singaporean and Indonesian—have all been influenced to varying degrees by the culinary genius of China. Ingredients such as noodles, tofu (bean curd), soy sauce, and fresh bean sprouts are just some Chinese ingredients found in almost all of tropical Asia.

In addition to a wide range of Chinese seasonings and local spices and herbs, the food of most of tropical Asia is full of aromatic roots and members of the onion family (onions, garlic, shallots, chives). The huge botanical family of gingers includes many edible varieties, including the common ginger known throughout the world. Brilliant yellow turmeric, galangal root (used medicinally in Europe in the Middle Ages), and the edible pink bud of another wild ginger are all used fresh, their intense flavor adding to regional cuisines.

Singapore, a tiny but vibrant metropolis just north of the equator and off the southern tip of the Malay Peninsula, is largely populated by ethnic Chinese. In addition to its wide array of southern Chinese dishes, Singapore offers the food of its indigenous Malays, and the flavors of the Indian Subcontinent brought by 19th-century migrants. If there has to be one place in all of tropical Asia where it is possible to enjoy both traditional and creative new dishes from the entire region, it is Singapore. Often well traveled and, for the most part, familiar with international cuisine, Singapore's chefs have actively worked at evolving a new pan-Asian cuisine based on the wide range of local dishes already found in the country. It's not just East meets West, but East meets East in Singapore, where the philosophy seems to be "if an ingredient works, it doesn't matter where it's from, just use it."

The creation of a cross-cultural cuisine is nothing new for Singapore. More than a century ago, the blending of Chinese and Malay cultures and cuisines in Singapore and the

Malaysian centers of Malacca and Penang led to the evolution of what is known locally as Nonya food. This clever blending of Chinese ingredients and cooking styles with the local spices, herbs, and fruits is without doubt one of tropical Asia's finest culinary offerings.

The cuisine of Malaysia (where the major races are Malay, Chinese, and Indian) shares much with neighboring Singapore and with Indonesia. Both Malay and Indonesian food (particularly that of Sumatra) are robustly spiced and enlivened with chilies. Red or green finger-length chilies, dried chilies and bird's-eye chilies all have their individual flavor, fragrance and color, and are used accordingly.

Of all the Indonesian islands, it is Bali that has most enchanted the world. With its incredible physical beauty and unique culture that is an integral part of daily life and not just something paraded for tourists, Bali is also home to a distinctive cuisine. And because some of its chefs—like the tourists—come from around the world to work side-by-side with Balinese chefs, Bali has become another center where a creative new cuisine based on traditional dishes is evolving.

Many of the fresh herbs which enhance the food of Malaysia and Indonesia also add their almost head-spinning aromas to the foods of Thailand and Vietnam. Redolent of the jungle, they include lemongrass, kaffir lime leaf, Indonesian salam leaf, a range of basils, fresh coriander leaves (cilantro), regular mint, long-stemmed or "Vietnamese mint" (also known as laksa leaf or polygonum) and pandanus leaves.

The cuisines of Thailand and Vietnam are admired throughout tropical Asia, and some of its most distinctive ingredients, such as salty, pungent fish sauce, are borrowed by neighboring cooks. Thailand has several different regional cuisines but, overall, the food can be described as intensely flavorful. It is often hot, yet mild dishes soothed by coconut milk or reflecting Chinese origins can also be found. Lovers of fresh vegetables, the Thais are masters at producing superb salads. In Vietnam, salads may consist of a large platter of fresh herbs which are eaten together with cooked food ranging from fresh or deep-fried spring rolls to grilled meats. Less spicy than the cuisine of Thailand, Vietnamese food is generally fragrant, sometimes slightly sweet, and as it is rarely deep-fried—ideal for health-conscious food lovers.

To discover more of the fresh new flavors of tropical Asia, turn the pages of this book, choose a recipe or two, visit your nearest Asian market, then start cooking. Decorate your table with a piece of batik cloth or a sari, scatter it with orchids or perfumed flowers, put on a CD of haunting gamelan music, light an incense stick, and enjoy the sensations of tropical Asia.

essential ingredients

Banana buds, the unopened flowers of the banana plant, taste like artichokes and are a popular salad ingredient in Asia. To prepare them, remove the outer petals of the bud, quarter the tender heart and slice it length-wise. If not using immediately, soak the slices in cold water or sprinkle lime juice over them to prevent discoloration. Crisp cabbage leaves make a reasonable substitute.

Bean sprouts grown from mung beans are widely used in Tropical Asian cuisines. Mung bean sprouts have long thin bodies with a light flavor and nice crunch. They can be eaten raw, but are often cooked very briefly to retain their crunch. Soybean sprouts are available but are less common. Purchase sprouts fresh as they lose their crisp texture quickly. They will keep for a few days, however, if kept in the refrigerator immersed in a tub of water.

Candlenuts are waxy, cream-colored nuts similar in size and texture to macadamia nuts, which can be used as a substitute, although less-expensive raw almonds or cashews will also do. Candlenuts are never eaten raw or on their own, but are chopped, ground and cooked with seasonings and then added to curries and spice pastes for flavor and texture. The raw nuts go rancid quickly because of their high oil content, so buy them in small quantities and keep them refrigerated.

Cardamom pods are used to flavor curries and desserts—giving foods a heady, sweet aroma. The fibrous, straw-colored pods enclose 15–20 intensely aromatic black seeds. Whole pods are bruised lightly with a cleaver or a pestle before use. Do not buy ground cardamom as it is virtually flavorless compared with the heavenly fragrance of the freshly roasted and ground whole spice. Cardamom pods are available in health food stores and Indian grocers.

Carom seeds are derived from the same family as cumin and parsley, and are known as bishop's weed in the West and *ajwain* in India. The seeds are similar in appearance and flavor to caraway seeds, but with strong overtones of thyme. Look for the seeds in Indian specialty stores; it is worth trying to locate this spice as its use makes a subtle difference to the final flavor of many dishes. If unavailable, substitute dried thyme.

Thai basil (*horapa*)

Lemon basil (*mangkak*)

Basil is used as a seasoning and garnish in Tropical Asian cuisines. The commonly used basil in Asia is **Thai basil** or *horapa*. It is fairly similar to European and American sweet basil and is used as a seasoning and sprigs of it are often added to platters of fresh raw vegetables. **Lemon basil** or *manglak*, often used in soups and salads, is similar to *horapa* but paler and with a distinctive lemony fragrance. Thai basils are available in Asian food stores and many supermarkets. Sweet Italian basil makes an acceptable substitute.

Dried chillies

Fresh chillies

Bird's-eye chillies

Chilies are used throughout Asia. The commonly-used fresh green and red **finger–length chilies** are moderately hot. Tiny red, green or yellow-orange **bird's–eye chilies** are very hot, designed for strong palates. **Dried chilies** are usually cut into lengths and soaked in warm water to soften before use. They have a very different flavor from fresh chilies. To reduce the heat, cut open and discard some or all of the chili seeds before preparation.

Chinese chives, sometimes referred to as garlic chives, have flattened leaves and resemble thin green onions. They have a strong garlicky flavor and are often added to noodle or stir-fried vegetable dishes during the final stages of cooking. Substitute green onions, although their flavor is more mild.

Choy sum, also known as Chinese greens or Chinese flowering cabbage, is a leafy green vegetable with crunchy stems. Available in Asian markets, *choy sum* is now increasingly available in Western supermarkets too. Substitute any other crisp leafy greens, like bok choy.

Chinese rice wine is added to marinades and stir-fried dishes in very much the same way that sherry is used in Western cooking. Substitute Japanese sake or dry sherry.

Coconut milk or **cream** is available fresh or canned and in packets which are quick, convenient and quite tasty. Canned or packet coconut cream and milk comes in various consistencies, depending on the brand and you will need to try them out and adjust the thickness by adding water as needed. In general, add 1 cup of water to 1 cup of canned or packet coconut cream to obtain thick coconut milk, and 2 cups of water to 1 cup of coconut cream to obtain thin coconut milk. **Desiccated coconut** is grated coconut flesh that has been finely ground and dried. Sweetened and unsweetened coconut flakes of several sizes are sold in packets, usually in the baking section of supermarkets.

Coriander leaves, also known as cilantro are used as a herb and garnish. Fresh coriander leaves should keep for 5 to 6 days if you wash and dry the leaves thoroughly before placing them in a plastic bag.

Coriander seeds are round and beige. When ground they release a warm, nutty, slightly citrus-like aroma. Whole coriander seeds have a stronger flavor than ground coriander powder, although the latter may also be used.

Cumin seeds are pale brown to black in color and have thin ridges on the outside. They impart an earthy flavor and are used whole, or roasted and ground. Cumin seeds are usually partnered with coriander seeds in basic spice mixes, and are often dry-roasted or fried in oil to intensify their flavor. Cumin seeds are believed to aid digestion and are used in most Indian spice blends.

Curry leaves are an important herb in southern Indian cooking. The small, dark green leaf has a distinctive flavor which is sadly missing from the dried herb. When a sprig of curry leaves is called for in a recipe, this usually means 8–12 individual leaves. Curry leaves are available in Indian shops—dried leaves are not nearly as flavorful as fresh ones.

Curry powder is a commercial spice blend that generally includes cumin, coriander, turmeric, ginger, cinnamon and cloves. Different combinations vary in color and flavor and are used for different types of curries—meat, fish or chicken. Use an all-purpose blend if a specific curry powder is not available. Store in an airtight container

in the refrigerator after opening, and purchase in small quantities as it loses its aroma over time.

Daikon radishes are large and juicy root vegetables also known as "white carrots" or "white radishes." They are juicy but bland, unlike the smaller red radish. They can grow to a length of 15 in (40 cm) or more. Choose firm and heavy daikons without any bruises on them. Scrub or peel the skin before you grate or slice the flesh.

Dal is often spelled "dhal" in English and this term covers a variety of dried lentils. Three types are commonly used: Black gram lentils (urad dal), which is sold either with its black skin still on (substitute with black lentils) or husked, when it is creamy white in color (substitute with white lentils); masoor dal, salmon-pink lentils; toor, tuvar or arhar dal, a pale yellow lentil which is smaller than the black gram. The various types of dal can usually be found in Indian stores, supermarkets and health food stores.

Dried black Chinese mushrooms are similar to shiitake mushrooms. They are normally sold dried, but are also available fresh in many places. The tough stems are usually discarded and only the caps are eaten. They must be reconstituted by soaking in hot water for 20 minutes or longer. These mushrooms vary in size, thickness and quality. Try to buy the thicker and larger ones for dishes that feature mushrooms as a main ingredient. Fresh shiitake or porcini mushrooms may be substituted.

Dried rice paper wrappers are made from a batter of rice flour, water and salt. They are steamed and dried in the sun on bamboo racks, which leaves a crosshatched imprint. Used to wrap a wide variety of spring rolls, dried rice paper wrappers must be moistened before using. Available in Asian food markets, they will keep for many months if stored in a cool, dark place.

Dried shrimp are used in sauces and sambals. They are tiny, orange-colored saltwater shrimp that have been sun-dried. They keep for several months and should be soaked in water for 5 minutes to soften slightly before use. Look for dried shrimp that are plump and avoid any grayish ones. Better quality shrimp are bright orange in color and fully shelled.

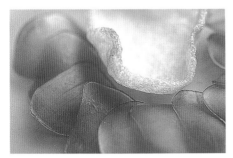

Dried shrimp crackers (*krupuk*) are dried crackers made from ground bits of shrimp, fish, vegetables and nuts mixed with various types of flour to make a very popular snack in Southeast Asia. They must be thoroughly dried in the sun or in an oven set on very low to remove the moisture before deep-frying in very hot oil for a few seconds, when they puff up spectacularly and become crispy. Store fried *krupuk* in an airtight container as they lose their crispness otherwise.

Dried shrimp paste is a dense mixture of fermented ground shrimp with a very strong odor that may be offensive to some. Also known by its Malay name, *belachan*, it is sold in blocks that range in color from caramel to dark brown. It should be roasted before use—either wrapped in foil and dry-roasted in a wok or skillet, or

roasted over an open flame on the end of a fork or in a spoon—to enhance its flavor and kill bacteria. In some recipes, dried shrimp paste is ground with the rest of the ingredients and fried in oil without toasting. Fish sauce may be substituted although it is very salty and the amount of salt in the recipe must be reduced if it is used.

Dried sweet Chinese sausages (*lap cheong*) are sweet, reddish sausages delicately perfumed with rice wine. They are used as an ingredient in stir-fries or braised dishes rather than being eaten on their own like European sausages. Sold in pairs, they keep almost indefinitely without refrigeration. Substitute any dried sweet sausage or meat jerky.

Fennel seeds are similar in appearance to cumin although slightly longer and fatter. Fennel seeds have a sweet fragrance that is similar to aniseed. The seeds are used whole or ground. They are available in health food stores and Indian grocers. If unavailable, substitute anise seed or cumin seed or caraway seeds or dill.

Fish sauce is a condiment used in almost every dish in Thailand and Vietnam, just as salt or soy sauce are used in other cuisines. Made from salted, fermented fish or shrimp, it has a very pungent, salty flavor in its pure form and is available in most supermarkets now in small bottles. Fish sauce is often combined with other ingredients such as sugar, garlic and lime juice to make various dipping sauces. Use sparingly and buy a quality brand for a better flavor. Refrigerate after opening.

Five spice powder is a blend of ground dried spices containing cinnamon, cloves, fennel, Sichuan pepper and star anise. It is sold in small containers in the spice section of most supermarkets.

Galangal is a fragrant root which looks like ginger but has a pink or yellow color. It imparts a distinctive fragrance and flavor to many Southeast Asian dishes. Try to find young, reddish galangal roots as they are more tender. Always peel and slice the root before grinding. Galangal is widely available fresh but also may be purchased dried, frozen and packed in water. Try to get the fresh root whenever possible as it is far more fragrant. If it is not available, use a combination of ginger and lemongrass as a substitute.

Garam masala is a blend of several strongly aromatic spices such as coriander, cumin, peppercorns and cardamom, designed to add flavor and fragrance to curries and meat dishes. Pre-blended *garam masala* can be bought from any store specializing in spices, including most health food stores. Store the ground powder in an airtight jar away from heat or sunlight.

Green pea shoots, also known as *dou miao*, are the immature tips or shoots of the snow pea and sugar pea, and are plucked as the crop of peas keeps growing and maturing. Pea shoots are enjoyed as a leafy green vegetable, and fetch an even higher price that the actual peas. Any sort of tender green sprouts may be substituted.

Hoisin sauce consists of fermented soybeans, garlic, chilies, and vinegar. The sauce is thick and dark and has as sweet, salty flavor. Hoisin sauce keeps well only when refrigerated after opening so it is best to buy a small jar or bottle and replenish with fresh supplies when needed. Commercially bottled or canned hoisin sauce is available in most grocery stores. Soy sauce or black bean sauce with sugar added can be used as a substitute.

Jicama (*bangkuang*) is a crunchy and juicy white tuber similar in texture and flavor to a sweet potato although more crunchy. Look for it in the produce section of supermarkets. Chayote or daikon radish may be substituted.

Kaffir lime leaves are added whole to curries, or finely shredded and added to salads, giving them a wonderfully tangy flavor. They are available frozen or dried in Asian food stores. Fresh or frozen leaves are far more flavorful than dried ones.

Laksa leaves, also called polygonum or Vietnamese mint, are traditionally added to spicy laksa soup dishes. The spear-shaped leaves wilt quickly once they are plucked from the stem. They have an intense

fragrance reminiscent of lemon with a hint of eucalyptus. There is no real substitute, but a mixture of spearmint and coriander leaves or basil does approximate the flavor and fragrance.

Lemongrass is a fragrant, lemony stalk that is either bruised and used whole in soups or curries, or sliced and ground as part of a basic spice paste. It is usually sold in bunches of 3 to 4 stems in supermarkets. The tough outer layers and green sheath should be peeled away and only the tender inner part of the thick lower third of the stem used. Always slice the stem before grinding to get a smooth paste. Fresh lemongrass is widely available now in most supermarkets and is much better than dried or frozen lemongrass.

Nori, also referred to as laver or seaweed, is toasted, crisp and sold in thin, dark green sheets of varying sizes. These sheets are used for wrapping sushi. Nori is also available as thinly shredded strips or flakes, both of which are used as a garnish served with rice. Sold in cellophane wrappers in most supermarkets.

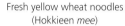

| Fresh yellow wheat noodles (Hokkieen *mee*) | Fresh flat rice noodles (*kway teow*) | Fresh laksa noodles (Rice noodles) | Dried rice vermicelli (*beehoon*) | Dried glass noodles (*tanghoon*) |

Noodles are a universal favorite in Asia. Both fresh and dried noodles made from either wheat, rice or mung bean flour are eaten. **Fresh yellow wheat noodles** (Hokkien *mee*) are heavy, spaghetti-like noodles made from wheat flour and egg. Substitute dried ramen or spaghetti. **Fresh flat rice noodles** (*kway teow*) are ribbon-like noodles about 1/2 in (12 mm) wide, used in soups or fried. Substitute dried rice stick noodles. **Fresh laksa noodles** are round like white spaghetti, but are made from rice flour and traditionally served in laksa soups. Substitute rice sticks or vermicelli. **Dried rice vermicelli** (*beehoon*) are very fine rice threads that must be blanched in boiling water to soften before use. **Dried glass noodles** (*tang hoon*), made from mung beans, are fine white strands that are generally used in soups. They are also called "cellophane" or "transparent" noodles, both accurate descriptions of their appearance after soaking. Both fresh and dried noodles should be blanched in boiling water before cooking to rinse and revive them—use a pair of long chopsticks to keep them from sticking together.

Nutmeg is the inner kernel of the fruit of the nutmeg tree. The lacy covering wrapped around the nutmeg is another spice—mace. Always grate whole nutmeg just before using as the powdered spice loses its fragrance quickly. Whole nutmegs keep almost indefinitely. Use ground nutmeg if you cannot find whole ones.

Oyster sauce is the rich, thick and dark extract of dried oysters. It is frequently added to stir-fried vegetable and meat dishes, and must be refrigerated once the bottle is opened. Expensive versions made with abalone and vegetarian versions made from mushrooms are also available. To shop for the best oyster sauce, look for a rich, thick, dark brown sauce with a strong oyster flavor. Check the ingredients listed on the bottle as some brands are loaded with MSG.

Palm sugar is sold as a block or cylinder made from the dried sap of the coconut or arenga sugar palm. It varies in color from gold to light brown and has a caramel taste. To measure, palm sugar should be shaved or melted in a microwave oven. Substitute dark brown sugar or maple sugar.

Pandanus leaves impart a subtle fragrance and a green color to dishes. They are usually tied in a knot and then added to a liquid recipe, but removed later after cooking. Bottled pandanus extract can be used in desserts, but if fresh or dried pandanus leaves are not available, omit them from savory dishes. Vanilla essence may be substituted in dessert recipes.

Paneer is a very mild-tasting Indian cheese like cottage cheese which is made by mixing milk with vinegar to form a curd, then draining the curd through a cloth and leaving it to set for a few hours under a heavy weight. Vegetarians may prefer to substitute firm tofu in place of paneer, and cream cheese or ricotta cheese may be substituted.

Pickled Sichuan vegetables, also known as *zha cai*, are the large roots of mustard greens that have been preserved with salt, garlic and plenty of hot chili. The whole vegetable is about the size of a closed fist. It has a pungent flavor and a crisp texture. Use sparingly in stir-fry dishes with pork or chicken, or slice thinly and add to soups. Sold loose or vacuum packed in plastic bags, but also available in cans. Look for it in Asian markets.

Preserved salted mustard cabbage (*kiam chye*) is used in some Chinese and Nonya dishes. It is a sour and salty vegetable that is frequently used in soups. Soak the heavily salted cabbage in water for 15 minutes to remove some of the saltiness, repeating if necessary. The taste is similar to salty sauerkraut, which makes a good substitute. It is sold in jars or plastic packets in Chinese food stores.

Saffron is the world's most expensive spice. The dried strands are usually infused in warm milk before being added to rice and dessert dishes. Store saffron in the freezer as it loses its fragrance quickly, and never buy powdered saffron if you want the true aroma of this spice. Available in the spice section of gourmet shops.

Salam leaves, from a tree belonging to the cassia family, are used in the same way bay leaves are used in Western cooking—to add a complex earthy fragrance to dishes. If unavailable, omit them from the recipe as there is no good substitute.

Sesame seeds are commonly pan-roasted to bring out their nutty flavor before being added to dishes. You can buy them already roasted or raw and then roast them yourselves in a dry skillet, moving them around so that they turn golden brown and do not burn. Black sesame seeds have a slightly bitter flavor and are sometimes used for decoration.

Sesame oil is extracted from roasted (darker oil) or raw (lighter oil) sesame seeds.

It is added to dishes in small quantities as a final touch for its strong nutty flavor and delicate fragrance. It is never used on its own as a frying medium as high heat turns it bitter.

Soy sauce is brewed from soybeans and wheat fermented with salt. It is salty and used as a table dip and cooking seasoning. **Dark soy sauce** is denser and less salty than regular soy sauce. It adds a smoky flavor to dishes. **Sweet Indonesian soy sauce** (*kecap manis*) is much sweeter and thicker than normal soy sauce. It has palm sugar and cane molasses added. Sweet Chinese soy sauce may be substituted or you can just add dark brown sugar to regular soy sauce. Try to find Indonesian *kecap manis* because it has a distinctive flavor.

Star anise is an 8-pointed dried pod encasing shiny black seeds with a strong aniseed (licorice) flavor. The whole spice is usually used when cooking sauces or curries and is discarded before serving. Whole star anise keeps for a year in an airtight container. It is available in Asian food markets.

Tamarind is a fruit originally from Africa and is used in many cuisines around the world today. It is often sold dried still encased inside its long, narrow tree pod. The pulp is often sold in jars or plastic packets already shelled, with seeds removed. It is used as a fruity souring agent in the form of a juice. To obtain tamarind juice, mash 1 part pulp in 2 parts warm water until the dried fruit dissolves and then strain. Discard the seeds or fibers. If using cleaned tamarind pulp, slightly reduce the amounts called for in the recipes. The dried pulp keeps indefinitely in an airtight container.

Tempeh or fermented soybean cakes, a Javanese creation, are made of compressed, lightly fermented soybeans that have a delicious nutty flavor. They can be fried, steamed or baked and are a rich source of protein, riboflavin, calcium and iron. They are low in cholesterol and sodium and are popular with health enthusiasts. They are sold in most health food stores and many supermarkets—plain, marinated or smoked. Look for them in the refrigerator or freezer section.

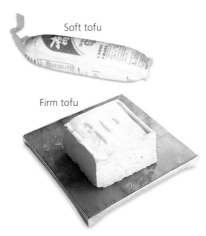

Soft tofu

Firm tofu

Tofu is rich in protein and amazingly versatile. Various types of tofu, originally introduced by the Chinese, are now used throughout the world. **Silken** or **soft tofu** has a very fine texture, high water content and tends to break easily. **Firm tofu** holds its shape better when cut or cooked and has a stronger, slightly sour taste. Pressed tofu (often confusingly labeled as firm tofu) has much of the moisture extracted and is therefore much firmer in texture and excellent for stir-fries. Small cubes of **deep-fried tofu** (*tau pok*) are added to slow-cooked dishes and some soups.

Turmeric is a root that looks like ginger but has a brighter yellow to orange color and a strong woody flavor. Turmeric has antiseptic and astringent qualities, and stains permanently, so scrub your knife blade, hands and chopping board immediately after handling. Purchase fresh turmeric root and keep leftovers in the freezer as the flavor fades after a few days. Substitute 1 teaspoon ground turmeric for 1 in (2.5 cm) of the fresh root.

Wakame is a type of seaweed with a pleasant chewy texture and subtle flavor. It is often used in soups and salads. Wakame is sold either dried (it looks like a mass of large crinkly tea leaves) or in salted form in plastic bags. Reconstitute the dried seaweed by soaking in water before use. The salted version should be rinsed before use.

Wonton wrappers are square or round wrappers made of flour, eggs and water. The thin ones are used for dumplings in soups while the thicker ones are used for frying. Sold in the refrigerated or freezer sections of supermarkets, frozen wrappers should be thawed to room temperature before use.

Yogurt is often vigorously stirred (use a hand-held mixer) to ensure the liquid whey is reincorporated with the curds; this is referred to as whipped yogurt. Some Indian dishes call for a solid yogurt called hung yogurt. The thicker curd is desired for its firm texture. You can obtain this by simply pouring off the liquid whey if it has already separated, or by placing it in a muslin cloth or paper-lined coffee filter and setting it over a jar or hanging it over the kitchen sink. The whey, or liquid, will drip out and leave behind the yogurt solids.

BASIC RECIPES

A delightful array of sambals, sauces, dips, chutneys and pickles

Fresh Pineapple Sambal

2 tablespoons oil
5 cloves garlic, sliced
4 small shallots, sliced
1 red finger-length chili, deseeded and sliced
1 bird's-eye chili, deseeded and sliced
1 cup (200 g) finely diced fresh pineapple
1 teaspoon dried shrimp paste (*belachan*), dry-roasted and crushed (see page 19)
½ teaspoon salt
½ teaspoon sugar

1 Heat the oil in a saucepan and add the garlic, shallots and chilies. Fry for about 4–5 minutes. Add the pineapple and stir-fry for another 5 minutes, then stir in the dried shrimp paste, salt and sugar, mixing well.

2 Remove from the heat, cool, then transfer to a mortar or blender and grind until smooth, adding a little water if necessary, to keep the blades turning. Transfer to small serving bowls. Serve as a dip with Shrimp and Chicken Satays (page 35).

Serves 4   Preparation time: 10 mins
Cooking time: 10 mins

Lemongrass Sambal

½ teaspoon dried shrimp paste (*belachan*), dry-roasted (see page 19)
1 tablespoon lime or lemon juice
2 teaspoons oil
½ teaspoon salt
Ground black pepper, to taste
8–10 small shallots, thinly sliced
6–8 stalks lemongrass, tender inner part of bottom third only, thinly sliced
10 kaffir lime leaves, finely sliced
1 red finger-length chili, deseeded and sliced
2–3 bird's-eye chilies, deseeded and sliced

Mix the dry-roasted dried shrimp paste with the lime juice, oil, salt and pepper until dissolved. Then add the remaining ingredients and mix well. Serve with Grilled Whole Snapper (page 107) and Spicy Grilled Fish Fillets (page 109).

Serves 4   Preparation time: 5 mins

Shrimp Paste Sambal

3 tablespoons oil
5 small shallots, finely sliced
2 cloves garlic, minced
6–8 red finger-length chilies, deseeded and finely sliced
1 tablespoon dried shrimp paste (*belachan*), dry-roasted (see page 19)
1 small tomato, finely chopped
1½ tablespoons sugar
½ teaspoon salt
¼ teaspoon ground black pepper

1 Heat the oil in a small pan and add the shallots, garlic, chilies, dried shrimp paste and tomato. Stir-fry over low-medium heat until fragrant, 3–4 minutes. Add the sugar, salt and pepper. Cook for another 10 minutes, stirring frequently to prevent the mixture from sticking.

2 Cool and blend coarsely before using. Use this sambal for Tropical Chicken Salad (page 62)

Serves 4   Preparation time: 10 mins
Cooking time: 15 mins.

Sambal Belachan

8–10 red finger-length chilies, deseeded and sliced
10 small shallots, sliced
1 tablespoon dried shrimp paste (*belachan*), dry-roasted (see page 19)
2 tablespoons fresh lime juice
1 teaspoon sugar
1 teaspoon salt
4 small limes (kalamansi limes), tops sliced off, or 1 regular lime, quartered

1 Grind all the ingredients to a paste in a mortar or blender, adding a little water if necessary to keep the blades turning.

2 Transfer to 4 small dipping saucers, add a lime to each portion and serve with Hokkien Noodles (page 72).

Serves 4   Preparation time: 5 mins

Chili Sambal with Lime

6 red finger-length chilies, deseeded and sliced
1 teaspoon dried shrimp paste (*belachan*), dry-roasted (see page 19)
4 small limes (kalamansi limes), or 1 regular lime, quartered

1 Pound or grind the chilies together with the dried shrimp paste to form a paste.

2 Divide between 4 small bowls and add a small lime to each bowl for squeezing into the sambal to taste. Serve in small dipping saucers with Singapore Seafood Laksa (page 60) and Sumatran Chicken Laksa (page 61).

Serves 4   Preparation time: 5 mins

Fragrant Sweet Soy Sambal

2 tablespoons oil
3 small shallots, sliced
1 clove garlic, sliced
2 red finger-length chilies, deseeded and sliced
1 teaspoon minced galangal root
1 teaspoon minced fresh ginger root
¼ tomato, chopped
1 tablespoon thick sweet soy sauce (*kecap manis*)
1 teaspoon sugar
1 teaspoon fresh lime juice
½ teaspoon salt
Pinch of ground black pepper

1 Heat the oil in a small pan and add the shallots and garlic. Stir-fry over low heat for 2 minutes, then add the remaining ingredients. Cook over low-medium heat, stirring frequently, for 8 minutes.

2 Grind to a paste in a mortar or blender, adding a little water if necessary to keep the blades turning. Serve with Fresh Summer Rolls (page 51).

Serves 4   Preparation time: 10 mins
Cooking time: 10 mins

Sweet Palm Sugar Sambal

3 tablespoons oil
6 small shallots, sliced
4–5 cloves garlic, minced
6–8 red finger-length chilies, deseeded and sliced
2 bird's-eye chilies, deseeded and sliced
1 small tomato, chopped
2 teaspoons shaved palm sugar or dark brown sugar
1 teaspoon dried shrimp paste (*belachan*), dry-roasted (see page 19)
1 teaspoon salt
¼ cup (60 ml) tomato ketchup
¼ cup (60 ml) water

1 Heat the oil in a small saucepan and add the shallots, garlic and chilies. Stir-fry over low-medium heat until fragrant, 3–4 minutes, then add the tomato, palm sugar and dried shrimp paste. Cook, stirring frequently, 5 minutes. Cool then grind to a paste in a mortar or blender, adding a little water if necessary to keep the blades turning.

2 Return to the pan, stir in the salt, tomato ketchup and water. Cook over low heat, stirring frequently for 10 minutes. Transfer to small dipping saucers and serve at room temperature. Serve with Coconut Rice with Assorted Side Dishes (page 73) and Balinese Mixed Vegetables with Crispy Tempeh (page 121).

Serves 4   Preparation time: 10 mins
Cooking time: 20 mins

Aromatic Basting Sauce

3 tablespoons oil
3–4 small shallots, sliced
2 cloves garlic, minced
1 teaspoon minced galangal root
1 teaspoon minced fresh ginger root
1 red finger-length chili, deseeded and sliced
1 bird's-eye chili, deseeded and sliced
1/2 cup (125 ml) vegetable or chicken stock
3 tablespoons thick sweet soy sauce (kecap manis)
1/2 teaspoon salt
1/2 teaspoon ground coriander
1/2 teaspoon ground cinnamon
1/2 teaspoon freshly grated nutmeg
1/2 teaspoon ground white pepper
1/8 teaspoon ground cloves
Salt, to taste

1 Heat the oil in a small saucepan and add the shallots, garlic, galangal, ginger and chilies. Stir-fry over low heat until softened and fragrant, 4–5 minutes. Add the remaining ingredients. Bring to a boil, reduce the heat and simmer until the sauce is reduced by about half, 8–10 minutes.

2 Cool, then transfer to a mortar or blender and grind to a paste, adding a little water if necessary to keep the blades turning. Transfer the sauce to a wide bowl. Use as a basting sauce for Vegetable and Tofu Brochettes (page 50).

Serves 4   Preparation time: 5 mins
Cooking time: 15 mins

Tamarind Mint Sauce

3 tablespoons chopped mint leaves
2 cloves garlic
3 bird's-eye chilies, deseeded
1 red finger-length chili, deseeded
1/2 teaspoon salt
1/4 teaspoon sugar
2 tablespoons tamarind pulp, mashed in 1/2 cup (125 ml) warm water and strained to obtain the juice
1 tablespoon chopped fresh coriander leaves (cilantro)
1 green onion (scallion), sliced

Grind the mint leaves, garlic, chilies, salt and sugar in a mortar or blender to form a paste, then combine with the tamarind juice, stir and garnish with the coriander leaves and green onion. Serve with Vegetable Samosas (page 38).

Serves 4   Preparation time: 5 mins

Sweet Chili Sauce

5 red finger-length chilies, deseeded and sliced
2 cloves garlic, sliced
2 tablespoons white vinegar
6 tablespoons water
2 tablespoons sugar
1/2 teaspoon salt, or to taste

This is a quickly prepared version of the standard bottled sweet chili sauce. Blend all the ingredients in a blender until smooth. Taste and add more sugar or salt if necessary. Serve as a dip with Crispy Fried Wontons (page 40).

Serves 4   Preparation time: 5 mins

Thai Sweet Chili Sauce

1/3 cup (65 g) sugar
2 teaspoons white vinegar
1 tablespoon fish sauce
1/4 cup (30 g) finely diced cucumber
1 tablespoon chopped dry-roasted cashew nuts
1 kaffir lime leaf, finely sliced
1 red finger-length chili, deseeded and sliced

1 Put the sugar, vinegar and fish sauce in a small pan and cook over low heat, stirring, until the sugar completely dissolves. Simmer until the mixture becomes a little thick, about 2 minutes.

2 Transfer to a bowl and leave to cool. Add the diced cucumber, cashew nuts, kaffir lime leaf and chili to the sauce. Stir to mix well. Serve with Thai Shrimp Cakes with Sweet Chili Sauce (page 47).

Serves 4   Preparation time: 5 mins
Cooking time: 5 mins

Peanut Satay Sauce

Peanut Satay Sauce

2 tablespoons oil
3 small shallots, finely sliced
2 cloves garlic, minced
2 red finger-length chilies, finely sliced
1/2 teaspoon dried shrimp paste (belachan), dry-roasted (see page 19)
2 kaffir lime leaves
1 1/2 teaspoons minced fresh ginger root
2 tablespoons shaved palm sugar
1 tablespoon tamarind pulp, soaked in 1/4 cup (60 ml) warm water, mashed and strained to obtain the juice
1 tablespoon sugar
1 teaspoon salt
Ground black pepper, to taste
1 cup (250 ml) water
3/4 cup (100 g) peanuts, dry-roasted, skinned and finely ground

1 Heat the oil in a saucepan and stir-fry the shallots, garlic, chilies, dried shrimp paste, kaffir lime leaves and ginger over low-medium heat until fragrant, about 4 minutes.

2 Add the palm sugar, tamarind juice, sugar, salt, pepper and water, stirring well. Add the ground peanuts, bring to a boil and simmer, stirring from time to time, until the sauce has thickened, about 15 minutes.

3 Discard the kaffir lime leaves. Transfer the sauce to a serving bowl and serve as a dip with Shrimp and Chicken Satays (page 35) and Fragrant Beef Satay (page 72).

Serves 4   Preparation time: 5 mins
Cooking time: 20 mins

Sesame Soy Dressing

¹/₄ cup (60 ml) salad oil (not olive oil)
1 tablespoon soy sauce
2 teaspoons rice vinegar
2 teaspoons sugar
2 teaspoons sesame oil
1 teaspoon minced garlic
1 teaspoon minced fresh ginger root
1 teaspoon finely chopped red finger-length
  chili
1 teaspoon mirin or sweet sherry
Salt and ground black pepper, to taste

Combine all the ingredients except the salt and pepper in a bowl, whisking to mix well. Taste and season as desired. Use as a dressing for blanched green beans (see page 108).

Serves 4   Preparation time: 5 mins

Coriander Mint Dip

1¹/₄-in (3-cm) fresh ginger root, sliced
6 cloves garlic, sliced
1 green finger-length chili, deseeded and sliced
1 cup (40 g) fresh coriander leaves and stems
  (cilantro)
1 cup (40 g) fresh mint leaves
2 tablespoons oil
1 teaspoon mustard seeds
1 teaspoon cumin seeds
1 small onion, peeled and sliced
10 curry leaves
1 small tomato, peeled and chopped
2 teaspoons curry powder
³/₄ cup (180 ml) coconut milk
¹/₂ teaspoon salt

1 Process the ginger, garlic, chili, coriander leaves and stems, and mint leaves to a fine paste in a mortar or blender, adding a little water if necessary to keep the blades turning. Heat the oil in a pan and add the mustard and cumin seeds. Stir-fry over medium heat until they crackle, then add the onion and curry leaves. Stir-fry until the onion softens, 3–4 minutes, then add the tomato and cook for another 5 minutes.
2 Add the blended paste and cook, stirring frequently, 4–5 minutes. Pour in the coconut milk, add the salt and bring slowly to a boil, stirring. Simmer uncovered until the sauce thickens, about 8 minutes. Taste and add more salt if desired. Serve in small bowls with Tuna Cakes with Fresh Herbs (page 49).

Serves 4   Preparation time: 10 mins
Cooking time: 25 mins

Sesame Dip

1 egg yolk
¹/₂ teaspoon Dijon mustard
1 teaspoon finely chopped fresh coriander
  leaves (cilantro)
4 teaspoons salad oil
1 teaspoon sesame oil
Large pinch of salt
Ground black pepper, to taste
1 finger-length chili, deseeded and sliced

1 Put the egg yolk, mustard and coriander leaves in a small bowl and whisk to mix.
2 Add the salad oil, a little at a time, whisking constantly until the sauce thickens. Add the sesame oil and whisk in, then season with salt and pepper to taste and garnish with the sliced chili. Serve as a dip with Vegetarian Potstickers (page 39).

Serves 4   Preparation time: 15 mins

Tamarind Avocado Dip

¹/₂ avocado
1 tablespoon tamarind pulp, soaked in ¹/₄ cup
  (60 ml) warm water, mashed and strained to
  obtain the juice
¹/₄ cup (60 ml) white vinegar
¹/₄ cup (60 ml) fish sauce
¹/₄ cup (60 ml) oil
1 tablespoon sugar
1 tablespoon honey
1 red finger-length chili, deseeded and sliced
1 clove garlic, minced

Grind all the ingredients to a paste in a mortar or blender, adding a little water if necessary to keep the blades turning. Serve with Fresh Summer Rolls (page 51).

Serves 4   Preparation time: 5 mins

Wasabi Mayonnaise Dip

1–2 teaspoons dry wasabi powder mixed
  with a little water to form a paste, or 1–2
  teaspoons prepared wasabi paste
¹/₂ cup (125 ml) mayonnaise

Combine the wasabi paste and mayonnaise in a small bowl and mix well. Serve with Sesame and Shrimp Crusted Tuna Chunks (page 108).

Serves 4   Preparation time: 5 mins

Fish Sauce Dip

2 tablespoons water
1 tablespoon fish sauce
1 tablespoon lime or lemon juice
1 tablespoon minced garlic
1 tablespoon finely sliced red chili
1 tablespoon minced fresh ginger root

Combine all the ingredients in a bowl, stirring to mix well. Transfer to a sauce bowl and set aside. Serve with Fresh Summer Rolls (page 51).

Serves 4   Preparation time: 5 mins

Fish Sauce Dip

Vindaloo Dip

8–10 dried red finger-length chilies, deseeded
    and cut into short lengths
2 teaspoons minced fresh ginger root
4 cloves garlic, minced
1 teaspoon brown mustard seeds
1 teaspoon ground turmeric
1 teaspoon coriander seeds
1 teaspoon black peppercorns
1 teaspoon cumin seeds
1 teaspoon *garam masala*
$1/2$ cup (125 ml) vinegar
$1/2$ cup (125 ml) boiling water
2 tablespoons oil
2 tablespoons tomato paste
1 teaspoon sugar
$1/2$ teaspoon salt

1 Combine the chilies, ginger, garlic and all the spices including the *garam masala* in a bowl. Add the vinegar and water and leave to soak for 2 hours.

2 Put the solids and just 1–2 tablespoons of the liquid in a mortar or blender and grind to a paste. Add the remaining liquid and mix to blend in.

3 Heat the oil in a small pan, add the blended spice mixture, tomato paste and sugar. Bring to a boil, stirring, then cook very gently, uncovered, for 15 minutes. Stir in the salt, then press the sauce through a sieve. Serve as a dip with Barbecued Jumbo Shrimp with Vindaloo Dip (page 98).

Serves 4   Preparation time: 10 mins + 2 hours
soaking time   Cooking time: 20 mins

Chili Mayonnaise Dip

2 tablespoons oil
2 small shallots, sliced
1 clove garlic, minced
2 tablespoons small dried shrimp, soaked in
    hot water for 10 minutes, drained
1–2 teaspoons dried chili flakes
1 teaspoon finely chopped palm sugar or soft
    brown sugar
2 teaspoons fish sauce

Pineapple Vanilla Jam; Papaya Clove Jam; and Rhubarb and Nutmeg Jam

1 tablespoon tamarind pulp, soaked in $1/4$ cup
    (60 ml) warm water, squeezed and strained
    to obtain the juice
$1/4$ cup (60 ml) mayonnaise
1 teaspoon fresh lime juice
Salt and pepper, to taste

1 Heat the oil in a small pan and stir-fry the shallots, garlic and dried shrimp over low-medium heat until cooked, about 4 minutes. Add the dried chili flakes, palm sugar, fish sauce and tamarind juice and stir until the sugar completely dissolves.

2 Cool, then grind to a paste in a mortar or blender, adding a little water if necessary to keep the blades turning. Combine the paste with the mayonnaise and lime juice, then add salt and pepper to taste. Serve as a dip with Fragrant Crab Cakes (page 34).

Serves 4   Preparation time: 10 mins
Cooking time: 10 mins

Pineapple Vanilla Jam

1 tablespoon pectin powder
1 cup (200 g) sugar
$2^1/2$ cups (500 g) finely diced fresh ripe
    pineapple
4 vanilla beans, split
1 pod star anise

1 Put the pectin in a small bowl and stir in 1 tablespoon of the sugar. Set aside.

2 Place the remaining sugar, pineapple, vanilla beans and star anise in a saucepan and bring slowly to a boil, stirring constantly. Boil without stirring until the mixture is thick, about 15 minutes, then add the pectin mix. Stir over low heat, 2 minutes, then remove from the heat. Remove the vanilla beans and star anise, then transfer the jam to a sterilized glass jar.

Serves 4   Preparation time: 5 mins
Cooking time: 20 mins

Papaya Clove Jam

1 tablespoon pectin powder
1 cup (200 g) sugar
3 cups (500 g) finely diced firm, ripe papaya
2 stalks lemongrass, tender inner part of
    bottom third only, finely sliced
1/4 cup (60 ml) lemon juice
1/2 teaspoon ground cloves

1 Put the pectin in a small bowl and stir in 1 tablespoon of the sugar. Set aside.

2 Place the remaining sugar, papaya, lemongrass, lemon juice and cloves in a saucepan and bring slowly to a boil, stirring constantly. Boil without stirring until the mixture is thick, about 15 minutes, then add the pectin mix. Stir over low heat, 2 minutes, then remove from the heat. Transfer to a sterilized glass jar.

Serves 4   Preparation time: 5 mins
Cooking time: 20 mins

Rhubarb and Nutmeg Jam

1 tablespoon pectin powder
1 cup (200 g) sugar
3 cups (500 g) finely diced rhubarb
1/2 teaspoon freshly grated nutmeg

1 Put the pectin in a small bowl and stir in 1 tablespoon of the sugar. Set aside.

2 Place the remaining sugar, rhubarb and nutmeg in a saucepan and bring slowly to a boil, stirring constantly. Boil without stirring until the mixture is thick, about 15 minutes, then add the pectin mix. Stir over low heat, 2 minutes, then remove from the heat and transfer to a sterilized glass jar.

Serves 4   Preparation time: 5 mins
Cooking time: 20 mins

Banana Chutney

2 teaspoons oil
1 teaspoon mustard seeds
10 curry leaves
2 dried red finger-length chilies, soaked in
    water for 5 minutes, coarsely sliced
2 ripe but firm bananas, coarsely mashed
6 tablespoons orange juice
1 teaspoon ground turmeric (optional)
Salt and black pepper, to taste

1 Heat the oil in a small pan and add the mustard seeds, curry leaves and dried chilies. Stir-fry until the seeds crackle, then add the banana and mix well with a wooden spoon, cooking for 1 minute. Stir in the orange juice, ground turmeric and season with salt and pepper.

2 Remove from the heat and allow to cool thoroughly. Chill in the refrigerator. Serve with Tuna Cakes with Fresh Herbs (page 49) and Naan Basket with Chutneys and Raita (page 79).

Serves 4   Preparation time: 5 mins + chilling time
Cooking time: 15 mins

Tomato Chutney

4–6 small ripe tomatoes, chopped
2 red finger-length chilies, deseeded and sliced
2 tablespoons oil
1 small onion, thinly sliced
1 teaspoon brown mustard seeds
10–12 curry leaves
1 tablespoon ground coriander
Salt and black pepper, to taste

1 Grind the tomatoes and chilies to a paste in a mortar or blender, adding a little water if necessary to keep the blades turning.

2 Heat the oil in a saucepan and stir-fry the onion, mustard seeds, curry leaves and ground coriander over low-medium heat for 2–3 minutes.

3 Add the processed mixture, stirring well. Bring to a boil, lower the heat and simmer uncovered for 10 minutes. Add salt and pepper to taste. Serve with Masala Dosai Rice Flour Pancakes (page 118).

Serves 4   Preparation time: 5 mins
Cooking time: 15 mins

Tomato Chutney

Fresh Coconut Chutney

Fresh Coconut Chutney

2¹/₂ cups (250 g) freshly grated or moistened
   unsweetened desiccated coconut
¹/₂ cup (20 g) fresh mint leaves
1 green finger-length chili, deseeded and sliced
1 teaspoon salt
¹/₃ cup (80 ml) water
2 tablespoons oil
1 teaspoon brown mustard seeds
8–10 curry leaves, sliced
¹/₂ small onion, finely sliced

1 Grind the coconut, mint leaves, chili, salt and
water to a paste in a mortar or blender. Set aside.
2 Heat the oil in a small saucepan and stir-fry
the mustard seeds, onion and curry leaves over
low-medium heat until the onion is soft, 3–4
minutes.
3 Pour the fried onions and spices over the
fresh chutney and stir to mix. Serve with Masala
Dosai Rice Flour Pancakes (page 118).

Serves 4   Preparation time: 5 mins
Cooking time: 5 mins

Green Chili Mango Chutney

1¹/₄ cups (200 g) peeled and diced unripe
   green mango (made from 1 large or 2 small
   mangoes)
2¹/₂ cups (250 g) freshly grated coconut or
   moistened unsweetened desiccated coconut
2–3 green finger-length chilies, deseeded and
   sliced
¹/₂ teaspoon salt
1¹/₂ tablespoons oil
¹/₂ teaspoon black gram lentils
¹/₂ teaspoon mustard seeds
1 sprig curry leaves
¹/₄ teaspoon asafoetida (optional)

1 Coarsley grind the diced mango, coconut,
chilies and salt, then set aside.
2 In a small saucepan, over a low flame, heat
the oil and stir-fry the black gram lentils until
golden brown. Add the mustard seeds and
curry leaves and stir-fry until the mustard seeds
pop. Add the asafoetida, if using, mix and
remove from the heat.
3 Transfer the fried spices to the ground

chutney and mix well. Serve with Naan Basket
with Chutneys and Raita (page 79).

Serves 4   Preparation time: 10 mins
Cooking time: 15 mins

Sweet Asian Pickles

1 cup (250 ml) water
¹/₂ cup (125 ml) white vinegar
3 tablespoons sugar
1 tablespoon coarse salt
1 small carrot, sliced into matchsticks
1 baby or Japanese cucumber, skin left on,
   sliced into matchsticks
¹/₃ cup (40 g) finely sliced red bell pepper
2–3 small shallots, thinly sliced
1 red finger-length chili, deseeded and sliced
   into thin strips

1 Bring the water, vinegar, sugar and salt to a
boil in a small saucepan, stirring until the sugar
and salt completely dissolves.
2 Put the sliced vegetables in a bowl and mix
well by hand. Pour over the hot vinegar mix
and leave to cool, then refrigerate 1–2 hours to
chill thoroughly. (If you prefer a more crunchy
version of this pickle, allow the vinegar mix to
cool before pouring over the vegetables.)

Serves 4   Preparation time: 10 mins + chilling time
Cooking time: 10 mins

Pineapple Cucumber Raita

³/₄ cup (180 ml) plain yogurt
¹/₄ teaspoon salt
Liberal sprinkling of ground white pepper
³/₄ teaspoon ground cumin
¹/₂ cup (65 g) finely diced cucumber
¹/₂ cup (100 g) finely diced pineapple

Combine the yogurt, salt, pepper and ground
cumin in a bowl, stirring to mix well. Add the
diced cucumber and pineapple. Mix well and
chill for at least 30 minutes. Serve with Chapati
Vegetable Wrap (page 124).

Serves 4   Preparation time: 10 mins
Chilling time: 30 mins

Pickled Cucumber

¹/₃ cup (65 g) sugar
2 tablespoons white vinegar
1 cup (250 ml) water
2 in (5 cm) fresh ginger root, smashed
1–1¹/₂ teaspoons salt
2 baby cucumbers, skin raked with a fork
5–8 green bird's-eye chilies, left whole, bruised
2 small shallots, thinly sliced

1 Bring the sugar, vinegar, water, ginger and salt to a boil in a saucepan. Simmer for 2 minutes, then allow to cool. Remove the ginger and transfer the liquid to a bowl.
2 Halve the cucumbers lengthwise, discard the seeds and cut across in ¹/₂-in (12 mm) slices. Add the cucumber, chilies and shallots to the cooled syrup, mixing well. Cover and refrigerate 2 hours before serving. Serve with Coconut Rice with Assorted Side Dishes (page 73).

Serves 4　Preparation time: 5 mins + 2 hours chilling time　Cooking time: 10 mins

Sushi Rice

1¹/₂ cups (300 g) uncooked short-grain Calrose or Japanese rice
2 cups (500 ml) water
1 piece *kombu* seaweed, 2¹/₂-in (6-cm) square
3 tablespoons rice vinegar
2 tablespoons sugar
1 tablespoon *mirin*
1 teaspoon salt

1 Put the rice, water and *kombu* in a pan, cover and bring to a boil. Discard the *kombu* and cover the saucepan, leaving the lid slightly open. Cook over medium heat until the water is completely absorbed, about 5 minutes. Cook over minimum heat for another 10 minutes. Wipe the inside of the saucepan lid, cover and remove from the heat. Let stand for 10 minutes.
2 Stir the rice vinegar, sugar, *mirin* and salt in a small bowl until the sugar and salt are dissolved. Transfer the cooked rice into a wide bowl and separate the grains gently with a wooden spoon, gradually sprinkling the rice vinegar mixture over the rice. Toss the rice gently until it has cooled slightly, 5 minutes. Set aside until completely cooled, about 20 minutes. This recipe makes 5 cups (500 g) cooked sushi rice.

Makes 3 cups (300 g) cooked sushi rice
Preparation time: 10 mins + standing time
Cooking time: 50 mins

Shallot Oil

3 small shallots, peeled and halved
¹/₂ small onion, peeled and sliced
3 in (7.5 cm) fresh ginger root, sliced
6 cloves garlic, peeled and smashed
2¹/₂ cups (625 ml) oil

1 Combine the shallots, onions, ginger, garlic and oil in a large pan and cook over medium heat until most of the ingredients are golden brown and fragrant.
2 Leave to cool, then pass through a sieve and pour the oil into a bottle.

Preparation time: 10 mins　Cooking time: 10 mins

Crispy Fried Garlic

20 cloves garlic
¹/₂ cup (125 ml) oil

1 Peel and mince the garlic.
2 Heat the oil in a skillet and stir-fry the minced garlic over low heat until golden brown. Drain and set aside to cool. Keep the fried garlic in a sealed jar.

Preparation time: 10 mins　Cooking time: 10 mins

Crispy Fried Shallots

12 small shallots
1 cup (250 ml) oil

1 Soak the shallots in salted water for 5 minutes, then peel and slice them thinly. Pat dry thoroughly with paper towels.
2 Heat the oil in a skillet and stir-fry the shallots over medium heat until golden brown and crispy. Drain and set aside to cool. Store in a sealed jar for up to 2–3 weeks.

Preparation time: 10 mins　Cooking time: 10 mins

Crispy Fried Shallots

appetizers

Fragrant crab cakes

If you can obtain fresh crabmeat for these excellent crab cakes, the result is sublime. But even with canned or frozen crabmeat, these herb-scented cakes accented with soy, sesame, fish sauce and chili sauce will have your guests coming back for more. The unusual dip which accompanies the cakes is an East-West blend of mayonnaise, dried shrimp, fish sauce and lime. This recipe is so good you may want to make double quantities and serve the crab cakes as a main course.

1 Process the fish in a food processor until it forms a fine paste. Add the crabmeat, herbs, soy sauce, sesame oil, fish sauce and hot sauce and pulse several times to mix well. Transfer the mixture to a bowl and stir in the diced bell pepper. (If the mixture seems too moist, stir in 2–3 tablespoons of breadcrumbs.) Shape the mixture to make 12 small patties. Dredge each patty in the flour, then dip into the beaten egg and coat well with the breadcrumbs. Refrigerate 30 minutes.

2 Heat 2 tablespoons of the oil and add half the crab cakes. Fry over medium heat, about 2–3 minutes on each side, until golden brown and cooked. Drain on paper towels and repeat with the remaining crab cakes. Serve hot with the Chili Mayonnaise Dip and garnish with watercress and roasted bell pepper strips, if desired.

4 oz (125 g) white-fleshed fish (such as snapper, bream or grouper), sliced
2 cups (240 g) cooked crabmeat
1 teaspoon finely chopped garlic
1 teaspoon finely chopped fresh ginger root
1 stalk lemongrass, tender inner part of bottom third only, finely chopped
¼ cup (10 g) finely sliced Thai basil
¼ cup (10 g) finely chopped fresh coriander leaves (cilantro)
1 green onion (scallion), finely chopped
4 teaspoons soy sauce
4 teaspoons sesame oil
2 teaspoons fish sauce
1–2 teaspoons bottled hot sauce
½ cup (80 g) finely diced bell pepper
½ cup (75 g) all-purpose (plain) flour
1 egg, lightly beaten
1 cup (60 g) breadcrumbs
¼ cup (60 ml) oil
Fresh watercress, to garnish (optional)
1 roasted red bell pepper, cut into strips, to garnish (optional)
1 portion Chili Mayonnaise Dip (page 28), for dipping

Serves 4
Preparation time: 20 mins + refrigerating time
Cooking time: 10 mins

Shrimp and chicken satays

Satay in Southeast Asia ranges from simple skewers of grilled meat served with a dip of thick sweet soy sauce and sliced chilies to sophisticated versions like this. Chicken breast cubes and shrimp are marinated in an aromatic paste before being grilled and are served with a thick, slightly sweet Peanut Satay Sauce and an intriguing sweet-sour Fresh Pineapple Sambal. This makes a most impressive appetizer.

1 To prepare the Satay Marinade, heat the oil in a small pan and stir-fry the shallots, garlic, ginger, turmeric and lemongrass over low heat until fragrant and cooked, about 8 minutes. Cool, then blend to a paste. Transfer to a bowl and stir in the honey and salt. Set aside to cool, then stir in the chicken pieces and shrimp and marinate in the refrigerator for 3–4 hours.

2 Thread the marinated chicken pieces and shrimp on bamboo skewers. Grill on a grill pan, under a broiler or over very hot charcoal, turning to cook and brown all over, 1–2 minutes each side. Serve with dipping bowls of Peanut Satay Sauce and Fresh Pineapple Sambal on the side.

Serves 4   Preparation time: 20 mins + 3–4 hours marinating time   Cooking time: 20 mins

1 chicken breast (8 oz/250 g), cut into 1¹/₄-in (3-cm) cubes

1 lb (500 g) fresh shrimp, peeled, tail section left intact

15–18 bamboo skewers, soaked in water for 30 minutes

1 portion Peanut Satay Sauce (page 26), for dipping

1 portion Fresh Pineapple Sambal (page 24), for dipping

SATAY MARINADE

3 tablespoons oil

6 small shallots, sliced

5–6 cloves garlic, sliced

1 tablespoon chopped fresh ginger root

1 teaspoon ground turmeric

2 stalks lemongrass, tender inner part of bottom third only, sliced

2 teaspoons honey

1 teaspoon salt

NOTE: If you prefer to serve only one kind of satay, double the amount of the chicken or shrimp. Grill some skewered bell pepper strips or fresh chili peppers, with the seeds removed, if you fancy a really hot appetizer!

Seared seafood salad

This salad is perfect for lunch, or for a starter at dinner, and the Cilantro Dressing is excellent poured over any sort of grilled seafood.

10 fresh scallops
4 small squid, peeled
½ teaspoon salt
Liberal sprinkling of ground white pepper
1 tablespoon olive oil
8 arugula or lettuce leaves, washed and dried
2 kaffir lime leaves, finely sliced
2 small onions, thinly sliced
2 tablespoons finely sliced carrot
1 red finger-length chili, deseeded and finely sliced lengthwise
1 teaspoon sesame seeds, roasted until golden

CILANTRO DRESSING
⅓ cup (80 ml) fish sauce
3 tablespoons fresh lime juice
2 teaspoons finely chopped fresh coriander leaves (cilantro)
1 teaspoon sesame oil
1 red finger-length chili, deseeded and finely sliced
1 clove garlic, minced
1 teaspoon sugar
3 tablespoons extra virgin olive oil, or a combination of flavored oils (Garlic Oil and Orange/Lemon Oil—recipes below)
1 kaffir lime leaf, finely sliced

GARLIC OIL
Scant ½ cup (100 ml) oil
6 cloves garlic, smashed
Salt and pepper, to taste

ORANGE OR LEMON OIL
⅔ cup (150 ml) oil
2 tablespoons grated lemon rind or 3 tablespoons orange juice
1 bay leaf
Salt and pepper, to taste

1 To make the Garlic Oil, heat the ingredients over very low heat until the oil is flavorful and aromatic. Remove from the heat and set aside to cool, then store in a sealed jar.

2 Make the Orange or Lemon Oil by heating the ingredients over very low heat until the oil is flavorful and aromatic. Remove from the heat and set aside to cool, then store in a sealed jar.

3 Prepare the Cilantro Dressing by combining all the ingredients except the olive oil (or flavored oils) and kaffir lime leaf in a small bowl, stirring until the sugar completely dissolves. Put the olive (or flavored) oil in a separate bowl and add the mixture a few drops at a time, whisking constantly until the dressing starts to emulsify and thicken. Keep adding the oil gradually until it is all absorbed, then stir in the kaffir lime leaf and set the Cilantro Dressing aside.

4 Make a crosshatch pattern on the squid by cutting the bodies in half lengthwise. Score the soft inside of the squid pieces with diagonal lines using a very sharp knife, taking care not to cut right through the flesh. Turn the piece of squid and score diagonally across the lines already made, resulting in a crisscross pattern. Cut each squid half into bite-sized pieces.

5 Sprinkle the scallops and squid on both sides with salt and pepper. Heat half the oil in a wok and stir-fry the scallops over very high heat until they turn white, about 1 minute. Remove and drain on paper towels. Add the remaining oil and, when very hot, stir-fry the squid halves until they turn white, about 1½–2 minutes. Remove and drain on paper towels.

6 Arrange the arugula or lettuce leaves, kaffir lime leaves, onions, carrot and chili on a serving plate. Add the scallops and squid, drizzle with the Cilantro Dressing and sprinkle with sesame seeds.

Serves 4   Preparation time: 15 mins   Cooking time: 25 mins

2 cups (300 g) all-purpose (plain) flour, plus
  extra for kneading
2 tablespoons oil
½ cup (125 ml) water
Oil, for deep-frying
1 portion Tamarind Mint Sauce (page 26),
  for dipping

POTATO FILLING
2 tablespoons oil
2 teaspoons brown mustard seeds
1 small onion, sliced
1–2 green finger-length chilies, sliced
10–12 curry leaves, sliced
1 tablespoon curry powder
½ teaspoon minced garlic
½ teaspoon minced fresh ginger root
3 potatoes, boiled and diced
1 carrot, peeled and diced to yield 1¼ cups
  (150 g), blanched then drained
1 teaspoon salt
2 tablespoons chopped fresh coriander leaves
  (cilantro)

NOTE: The filling, with the potato coarsely
mashed before mixing with the seasonings, can
be served as a vegetable dish on its own.

Vegetable samosas

Samosas are a very popular snack in India, Sri Lanka and wherever Indian
communities are found. A simple pastry of flour, oil and water is used to
enclose a spicy filling—in this case, potato and carrot with herbs and
spices. A tart Tamarind Mint Sauce is the perfect dip for these morsels.

1 To make the Potato Filling, heat the oil in a saucepan and add the mustard seeds. Cook until
they start to crackle, then add the onion, chilies and curry leaves. Stir-fry over low-medium
heat until the onion turns golden. Add the curry powder, garlic and ginger. Stir for 30 seconds,
then add the potatoes and carrots. Stir to mix well. Transfer to a bowl and stir in the salt and
coriander leaves. Set aside.

2 Sift the flour into a mixing bowl. Make a well in the center and pour in the oil and water. Stir
to incorporate the liquid, then knead the dough on a floured board for about 10 minutes until
soft but not sticky, adding a little extra flour if needed. Divide the dough into small balls, then
flatten each ball of dough with your hand. Roll out the dough to form a thin disc about 5½ in
(14 cm) in diameter. Cut each disc in half.

3 Put 1 heaping teaspoon of the Potato Filling on each half disc. Moisten the outer edges of
the dough with water, then fold it around the filling, pressing the edges to seal firmly.

4 Heat the oil in a wok until hot. Deep-fry the samosas, a few at a time, until golden brown,
2–3 minutes. Drain on paper towels and serve hot with the Tamarind Mint Sauce.

Serves 4   Preparation time: 25 mins   Cooking time: 20 mins

Vegetarian potstickers

Inspired by Chinese meat-filled dumplings, these vegetarian potstickers are very quick to make if you use ready-made wonton wrappers rather than making your own dough. The eggplant filling is full of flavor, while the mayonnaise-like dip with Asian flavors of sesame oil and fresh coriander leaves is excellent. These potstickers are so good you may want to make a double portion.

1 Preheat the oven to 350°F (180°C). Brush the top of each eggplant with a little of the olive oil and sprinkle with salt, pepper and a little of the basil leaves. Cook in the preheated oven until soft, about 15 minutes. Cool, then peel and finely chop the eggplant and place in a bowl.

2 Heat the remaining oil and stir-fry the shallots over low-medium heat until transparent, 2–3 minutes. Add to the eggplant, along with the remaining basil leaves, coriander leaves and ground red pepper. Taste and add salt and pepper if needed.

3 Sprinkle a plate with the cornstarch. Moisten the edges of a wonton wrapper with a finger dipped in water. Place the wrapper on a clean work surface and put 1 heaping teaspoon of the eggplant mixture in the center of each wonton wrapper. Enclose the filling with the wrapper and pinch the edge together to seal. Place each dumpling on the floured plate as you work.

4 Heat the oil in a large non-stick skillet. When hot, add the dumplings, bottom side down and cook until golden brown, about 2 minutes. Add the water, cover the pan and cook until the water has evaporated, about 2 minutes. Transfer to a serving dish. Serve with the Sesame Dip.

2 long purple Asian eggplants, about 10 oz (300 g), halved lengthwise
1½ tablespoons olive oil
Salt and black pepper, to taste
2 tablespoons finely chopped fresh basil leaves
4 small shallots, finely sliced
2 teaspoons finely chopped fresh coriander leaves (cilantro)
Pinch of ground red pepper (cayenne)
2 teaspoons cornstarch
12 wonton wrappers
2 tablespoons oil, for frying
¹/₃ cup (80 ml) water
1 portion Sesame Dip (page 27), for dipping

Makes 12 potstickers
Preparation time: 25 mins
Cooking time: 30 mins

Rice paper rolls with fresh tuna

This unusual version of the popular Vietnamese rice paper rolls contains a mixture of fresh sashimi quality tuna with lashings of fragrant herbs and a luxurious sauce with a touch of aged brandy. The dipping sauce has plenty of garlic, deseeded chili (so it is quite mild), fish sauce and lime, making this a wonderfully piquant appetizer. This recipe can also be used to make chicken and shrimp rice paper rolls (see Note).

4 oz (125 g) fresh sashimi quality tuna
1/2 cup (20 g) finely chopped fresh coriander leaves (cilantro)
1/2 cup (25 g) finely chopped fresh Chinese celery or Italian parsley leaves
1/2 cup (20 g) finely chopped mint leaves
1/2 cup (20 g) finely chopped basil
4 tablespoons XO sauce, oil drained off (see note)
1 teaspoon pepper
2 teaspoons sugar
1/2 teaspoon sesame oil
10–12 dried rice paper wrappers (8 in/20 cm in diameter)

DIPPING SAUCE
1/4 cup (60 ml) fish sauce
1/4 cup (60 ml) lime or lemon juice
2 tablespoons minced garlic
1–2 red finger-length chilies, deseeded and finely chopped
2 1/2 tablespoons white vinegar
3/4 cup (180 ml) water

1 To make the Dipping Sauce, combine all the ingredients in a small bowl, stirring to mix well.

2 Put the tuna, herbs, XO sauce, pepper, sugar and sesame oil in a bowl and stir to mix well. Dip a dried rice paper wrapper in a bowl of warm water for a few seconds until it starts to soften. Remove and place on a piece of clean damp kitchen towel. Smooth the rice paper wrapper with your fingers. Repeat with a second dried rice paper wrapper.

3 Arrange about 2 tablespoons of the tuna mixture across the center of a rice paper wrapper, to within 3/4 in (2 cm) of each side. Roll up the rice paper wrapper, tucking in the edges to make a cigar shape and completely enclose the filling. Repeat with the remaining rice paper wrappers. Divide the rolls between 4 plates and put the Dipping Sauce into 4 separate sauce bowls. Serve immediately.

NOTE: XO sauce is a blend of dried shrimp, shallots, garlic, chili and aged brandy and is available bottled in Chinese grocers, but any sweet Asian sambal or sauce that contains dried shrimp, garlic and chili may also be used, adjust the amount of sauce to taste depending upon the amount of chili desired. An alternative to using fresh tuna as the filling is to use chicken and shrimp instead. Blanch 1 1/2 cups (300 g) ground chicken breast and 10 oz (300 g) peeled and cooked shrimp and substitute for the tuna in the recipe.

To save time, you may use bottled Thai sweet chili sauce which is also an ideal partner for these rice paper rolls.

Makes 10–12 rolls   Preparation time: 20 mins

Crispy fried wontons

These delicious dumplings are deep-fried until crispy and golden brown. Serve piping hot with a spicy Chili Sauce, the perfect counterpoint to the mild yet flavorful chicken filling.

2/3 cup (130 g) ground chicken
1 clove garlic, minced
1 1/2 teaspoons rice wine (or sherry)
1 1/2 teaspoons oyster sauce
Pinch of salt
Liberal sprinkling of ground white pepper
8 large wonton wrappers
1 egg yolk, stirred to mix
Oil, for deep-frying
1 portion Sweet Chili Sauce (page 26), for dipping

1 Combine the chicken, garlic, rice wine or sherry, oyster sauce, salt and pepper in a bowl. Mix well.

2 Place 1 wonton wrapper on a clean work surface (keep the remaining wrappers covered with a damp cloth to prevent from drying out). Brush the edges with the egg yolk. Put some of the chicken mixture in one corner of the wrapper, then fold over to enclose the filling and make a triangle, pressing firmly to seal. Set aside and repeat with the remaining wrappers and filling.

3 Heat the oil in a wok until hot. Add the dumplings and deep-fry until crispy and golden, aout 1 minute. Remove and drain on paper towels. Serve with a dipping bowl of Sweet Chili Sauce on the side.

Makes 8 dumplings   Preparation time: 20 mins   Cooking time: 10 mins

1¼ lbs (600 g) fresh jumbo shrimp, peeled and
   deveined
1 teaspoon salt
Liberal sprinkling of ground white pepper
1 teaspoon olive oil

NUTMEG MAYONNAISE
Pinch of gelatin powder
1½ teaspoons warm water
1 cup (250 ml) mayonnaise
2 teaspoons lemon juice
5 teaspoons cream or evaporated milk
½ teaspoon ground nutmeg
½ teaspoon black sesame seeds

Serves 4
Preparation time: 10 mins
Cooking time: 20 mins

Grilled jumbo shrimp

This pretty finger food is deceptively easy to make, and is suitable for
any type of party—whether your guests are sporting black ties and
gowns or kakis and summer dresses. Lightly seasoned shrimp are grilled
and served with a dollop of a creamy white mayonnaise that's studded
with small black sesame seeds.

1 To make the Nutmeg Mayonnaise, melt the gelatin in the warm water, then add to the
mayonnaise together with the lemon juice, cream and nutmeg. Refrigerate in a covered
container for at least 1 hour or up to 2 weeks before serving. When ready to serve, stir in the
sesame seeds; set aside.

2 Toss the shrimp well in the salt and pepper. Brush with olive oil and cook on a grill pan or
under a broiler until done, about 2–3 minutes per side. Divide between 4 plates and garnish
each serving with a portion of the Nutmeg Mayonnaise. Serve immediately.

Tempura oysters

These succulent oysters require a few extra steps, but the result is worth the effort. Serve them at a special party or to start off an elegant dinner, and use the freshest oysters available.

1 cake soft tofu (about 10 oz/300 g)
1 cup (7 oz/200 g) ground shrimp or fish, processed to a paste
Salt and pepper, to taste
1/2 teaspoon sugar, or to taste
Pinch of cornstarch
1/2 teaspoon sesame oil
3 tablespoons finely chopped fried bacon bits
15 freshly shucked oysters
1/2 cup (60 g) tempura flour
Oil, for deep-frying
1 lime, sliced, to garnish
Parsley sprigs, to garnish

CHILI SAUCE
1 tablespoon bottled hot sauce
2 tablespoons tomato ketchup
2 tablespoons fresh lime juice
1 tablespoon chopped coriander leaves (cilantro)
3 cloves garlic, minced

1 Make the Chili Sauce by combining all the ingredients in a bowl, stir well and set aside.
2 Pass the tofu through a fine sieve and add the shrimp or fish meat paste. Stir in the salt, pepper, sugar, cornstarch, sesame oil and fried bacon bits and mix well. Refrigerate the mixture for 2 hours before using.
3 Coat each oyster with some of the tofu paste to form a dumpling.
4 Coat each oyster dumpling with a layer of tempura flour, then deep-fry until golden brown. Drain on paper towels, transfer to a plate or back into their shells and drizzle Chili Sauce on top of each oyster. Garnish with lime slices and parsley sprigs.

Serves 4
Preparation time: 10 mins
Cooking time: 20 mins

Tropical sushi

These recipes are a creative Balinese interpretation of Japanese sushi. You could always try just one or two of these sushi if you don't have time to prepare them all.

SPICY CHICKEN AND MANGO SUSHI ROLLS
1³/₄ cups (175 g) Sushi Rice (page 31)
2 tablespoons oil
2 small shallots, sliced
4 cloves garlic, sliced
1 red finger-length chili, deseeded and sliced
1 bird's-eye chili, deseeded and sliced
¹/₂ teaspoon dried shrimp paste (*belachan*)
¹/₂ teaspoon salt
Liberal sprinkling of ground white pepper
¹/₄ cup (50 g) finely shredded cooked chicken breast
¹/₃ cup (50 g) thinly sliced firm ripe mango
2 sheets *nori* seaweed, 7 x 8 in (18 x 21 cm)

1 Make the Sushi Rice by following the recipe on page 31.

2 Heat the oil and stir-fry the shallots, garlic, both chilies and the dried shrimp paste over low-medium heat until soft and cooked, 7–8 minutes. Cool, then pound or process to a paste and set aside.

3 Lay a piece of plastic wrap on top of a bamboo sushi rolling mat. Wet your hands. Spread half the Sushi Rice in a rectangle measuring about 5 x 7 in (13 x 18 cm) across the plastic, pressing it firmly with a spoon and your hands to compact the rice slightly; make sure the rice is spread evenly. Spread half the spice paste in a thin line down the center of the rectangle. Place a sheet of *nori* on top of the rice, then top this with half the chicken and mango. Roll up firmly using the mat, to enclose the filling completely with the rice. Remove the roll from the mat, then carefully remove the plastic. Repeat with the remaining ingredients to make 1 more roll. Slice each roll with a sharp knife into 5–6 pieces. Serve with pickled ginger, wasabi and soy sauce.

Serves 4   Preparation time: 25 mins
Cooking time: 1 hour

SHRIMP SAMBAL SUSHI
1¹/₂ cups (150 g) Sushi Rice (page 31)
8 fresh shrimp, shells intact
1 tablespoon oil
2 small shallots, sliced
2 teaspoons chopped lemongrass (from inner part of thick end of stem)
1 small bird's-eye chili
¹/₂ teaspoon dried shrimp paste (*belachan*), dry-roasted
¹/₂ teaspoon salt
Liberal sprinkling of ground white pepper
1 kaffir lime leaf, finely sliced into threads
¹/₂ red finger-length chili, deseeded and finely sliced
5 cm (2 in) green onion (scallion) leaf part only, finely sliced

1 Make the Sushi Rice according to page 31.

2 Push a toothpick or part of a bamboo skewer through each shrimp, from the back of the head to the tail, to hold it straight during cooking. Bring 1 cup (250 ml) lightly salted water to a boil, add the shrimp and simmer 3 minutes. Drain, cool and peel the cooked shrimp and remove the dark vein. Cut down the underside of each with a sharp knife, then press gently with the palm of the hand to spread open or "butterfly" each shrimp. Set aside.

3 Process the oil, shallot, lemongrass, chili, dried shrimp paste, salt and pepper to a paste.

4 Divide the Sushi Rice into 8 portions and squeeze each firmly with wet hands to make a compact cylinder about 2 in (5 cm) long. Press with the side of the finger in the center of each piece of rice to make a slight depression. Fill with a little of the spice paste, a few kaffir lime leaf threads, thin slice each of chili and green onion. Top each portion with a shrimp and serve.

Serves 4   Preparation time: 25 mins
Cooking time: 1 hour

BALINESE NORI ROLLS
1 cup (100 g) Sushi Rice (page 31)
1 tablespoon oil
3 cloves garlic, chopped
2 teaspoons chopped fresh ginger root
2 teaspoons chopped turmeric root
¹/₂ teaspoon ground black pepper
2 tablespoons coconut milk
¹/₄ teaspoon salt
1 tablespoon finely sliced red chili
2 green beans, cut into thin strips, blanched
2 large spinach leaves, finely sliced
1 Chinese (Napa) cabbage leaf, finely shredded
1 tablespoon roasted desiccated coconut
2 teaspoons Crispy Fried Shallots (page 31)
¹/₄ teaspoon fresh lime juice
1 sheet *nori* seaweed, 7 x 8 in (18 x 21 cm)

1 Make the Sushi Rice according to page 31.

2 Heat the oil in a small saucepan. Add the garlic, ginger, turmeric and pepper. Stir-fry over low-medium heat until cooked, 6–8 minutes. Cool, then process to a paste. Return the paste to the pan, stir in the coconut milk and salt, and heat, stirring. Transfer the mixture to a large bowl and set aside to cool. Add the chili, green beans, spinach, cabbage, roasted coconut, Crispy Fried Shallots and lime juice to the paste and toss to mix well.

3 Lay a piece of plastic wrap on top of a bamboo sushi mat. Wet your hands. Spread half the Sushi Rice in a rectangle measuring about 5 x 7 in (13 x 18 cm) across the plastic, pressing it firmly with a spoon and your hands to compact the rice slightly; make sure the rice is spread evenly. Arrange the filling down the center of the rectangle. Roll up firmly using the mat to enclose the filling with the rice.

4 Remove the roll from the mat, then carefully remove the plastic and place the roll on the sheet of *nori*. Roll up firmly. Cut across with a sharp knife into 5–6 pieces before serving.

Serves 4   Preparation time: 25 mins
Cooking time: 1 hour

Oil, for deep-frying
Sprigs of fresh coriander leaves (cilantro),
   to garnish

KOFTA BALLS
1 tablespoon oil
1 teaspoon cumin seeds
1/2 small onion, finely sliced
1 teaspoon minced garlic
1 teaspoon minced fresh ginger root
3 potatoes, boiled and mashed
3 tablespoons curd cheese (paneer) or grated
   ricotta
2³/4 cups (200 g) spinach leaves, blanched 1
   minute, drained, squeezed dry and finely
   chopped
1/2 teaspoon *garam masala*
1/2 teaspoon salt
3 tablespoons chickpea flour (*besan*)

GRILLED EGGPLANT PURÉE
2 long Asian purple eggplants, (about
   10 oz/300 g)
1 teaspoon minced garlic
2 teaspoons curry powder
1/3 cup (80 ml) plain yogurt
1/4 teaspoon salt
1 tablespoon chopped fresh coriander leaves
   (cilantro)
1/2 tomato, finely diced

Serves 4
Preparation time: 20 mins
Cooking time: 25 mins

Spinach cheese kofta and grilled eggplant pureé

This dish consists of two tasty vegetarian starters: kofta balls
made from spinach, potato and a little curd cheese or paneer and an
accompaniment of Grilled Eggplant Purée (not shown in photo).

1 Prepare the Grilled Eggplant Purée first. Cook the eggplants under a very hot broiler or
toaster oven, turning until the skin turns black and the inside is tender. Cut the eggplants open
and scoop out the flesh, discarding the skins. Chop the flesh finely and mix with all the other
ingredients. Set aside.
2 Make the Kofta Balls by heating the oil in a pan and frying the cumin seeds until they begin
to crackle. Add the onion, garlic and ginger and stir-fry over low-medium heat until softened,
about 3 minutes. Add the potatoes, cheese, finely chopped spinach, *garam masala* and salt.
Stir-fry for 2 minutes, mixing thoroughly. Transfer to a bowl and stir in the chickpea flour. Cool,
then shape into balls about 1¹/4 in (3 cm) in diameter.
3 Heat the oil in a wok until very hot. Deep-fry the Kofta Balls, turning until golden brown all
over, about 2 minutes. Drain on paper towels and serve accompanied by the Grilled Eggplant
Purée. Garnish with sprigs of coriander leaves.

Thai shrimp cakes with sweet chili sauce

Deep-fried shrimp or fish cakes are always popular. Thai red curry paste (which can be bought ready-made) and other typical Thai seasonings including fish sauce, kaffir lime leaf and garlic make the basic mixture of fish and shrimp really flavorful, while the accompanying sauce adds a touch of sweetness and heat.

1 lb (500 g) fresh shrimp, peeled and deveined
7 oz (200 g) boneless white fish fillets
  (snapper, grouper, bream), sliced
1 egg, lightly beaten
1–2 tablespoons red Thai curry paste
1 tablespoon finely sliced coriander (cilantro)
  roots and stems
2 tablespoons fish sauce
1 teaspoon baking soda
2 teaspoons sugar
1/2 teaspoon salt
1/2 teaspoon ground white pepper
3 cloves garlic, minced
1 kaffir lime leaf, finely sliced
3 green beans, thinly sliced
Oil, for deep-frying
1 portion Thai Sweet Chili Sauce (page 26),
  for serving

Serves 4
Preparation time: 20 mins
Cooking time: 15 mins

1 Pulse the shrimp and fish in a food processor until finely blended. Transfer to a mixing bowl. Fill a larger bowl with ice and set the bowl containing the shrimp mixture in the ice. Stir in the egg, curry paste, fish sauce, baking soda, sugar, salt, pepper, garlic, kaffir lime leaf and green beans, and mix well.

2 Wet your hands and shape about 2 tablespoons of the mixture into a ball, then flatten slightly to make a cake about 3/4-in (2-cm) thick. (The shrimp cakes will swell during frying because of the baking soda.)

3 Heat the oil in a wok. When hot, fry the shrimp cakes, a few at a time, until golden brown on both sides and cooked, 3–4 minutes. Drain on paper towels and serve hot with the Thai Sweet Chili Sauce.

1 in (2.5 cm) fresh ginger root, sliced
2 cloves garlic, minced
1 teaspoon salt
1 tablespoon fresh lime juice
2 teaspoons ground turmeric
1 teaspoon ground red pepper (cayenne)
1¼ lbs (600 g) skinned and deboned mackerel
    or swordfish, cut into 1¾-in (4-cm) cubes
1–2 tablespoons oil
Pandanus leaves, for wrapping fish
1 lime, cut into wedges

Serves 4
Preparation time: 10 mins + marinating time
Cooking time: 10 mins

Grilled fish nuggets

Jack fish and the related trevally are both ideal for this recipe of marinated grilled fish nuggets, although you could also use Spanish mackerel or swordfish. If you are not serving other substantial dishes, you may want to double the amount as the flavor is so good that the fish nuggets will disappear quickly!

1 Pound or process the ginger, garlic and salt together to make a paste, adding some of the lime juice if needed. Transfer to a bowl and stir in the lime juice, ground turmeric and ground red pepper. Add the fish cubes and toss to coat well. Cover and marinate in the refrigerator for 2–3 hours.

2 Brush the fish cubes with oil, loosely wrap them in the pandanus leaves and cook on a grill pan or under a broiler, turning, until golden brown, about 4 minutes on each side. Test with the tip of a sharp knife to make sure the fish is white in the center. Serve hot with lime wedges.

Tuna cakes with fresh herbs

Most fish cakes combine flaked fresh fish with mashed potato, but this unusual version encases a lightly seasoned mixture of canned tuna in a simple homemade pastry. The flavor of the tuna cakes is enhanced by a Coriander Mint Dip rich in fresh herbs, and an easily made fresh Banana Chutney.

1 cup (150 g) flour
Pinch of salt
¹/₃ cup (80 ml) water
1 tablespoon oil
1 portion Banana Chutney (page 29), to serve
1 portion Coriander Mint Dip (page 27), to serve

TUNA FILLING
²/₃ cup (100 g) drained canned tuna
2 tablespoons finely sliced onion
2 tablespoons finely chopped fresh coriander leaves (cilantro)
2 tablespoons freshly grated or moistened desiccated coconut
2 teaspoons fresh lime juice
Salt, to taste

1 Preheat the oven to 350°F (180°C).

2 Prepare the Tuna Filling by combining all the ingredients in a bowl, mixing well. Set aside.

3 Combine the flour, salt and water in a bowl. Knead for 5 minutes to make a pliable dough. Divide into 8 balls, then flatten each ball with the palm of your hand. Press with the thumbs and fingers to make each ball into a circle about 3¹/₄ in (8 cm) in diameter. Fill each circle with one-eighth of the Tuna Filling, then lift up the sides, pleating and squeezing them to the center to enclose the filling. Flatten gently into a cake about 2 in (5 cm) in diameter.

4 Heat the oil in a large skillet and sear the tuna cakes until golden brown, about 1¹/₂ minutes on each side. Transfer the tuna cakes to a baking tray and bake in the preheated oven for 8 minutes.

5 Serve the tuna cakes with Banana Chutney and Coriander Mint Dip.

Serves 4   Preparation time: 30 mins
Cooking time: 15 mins

Vegetable and tofu brochettes

These skewers of zucchini, bell pepper, onion, mushroom and tofu are ideal for vegetarians, and are equally good served with barbecued meat or poultry. The Aromatic Basting Sauce is accented with cinnamon, coriander, nutmeg and cloves for a truly tropical flavor.

1 portion Aromatic Basting Sauce (page 26)
8 bamboo skewers
1 medium zucchini, cut into 8 slices, each ³/₄-in (2-cm) thick
1 bell pepper, cut into 8 pieces, each about ³/₄-in (2-cm) square
1 small onion, cut into 8 wedges
8 button mushrooms, stems discarded
1–2 cakes firm tofu (10 oz/300 g per cake), cut into 16 pieces about ³/₄-in (2-cm) square
2 tablespoons coriander seeds, lightly roasted and coarsely crushed

1 Make the Aromatic Basting Sauce by following the recipe on page 26.

2 Thread 1 piece each of zucchini, bell pepper, onion, mushroom and tofu onto each skewer. Coat the skewers with the Aromatic Basting Sauce. Sprinkle each skewer with the coarsely crushed coriander seeds and grill under a broiler or on a hot fire, turning several times, until cooked.

NOTE: Do not grind the coriander seeds finely. Pound with a pestle or pulse a few times in a spice grinder. Alternatively, put the roasted seeds in a small plastic bag and roll with a rolling pin.

Serves 4
Preparation time: 10 mins
Cooking time: 25 mins

1 small carrot, peeled and sliced into long
   strips, blanched and drained
1 cup (100 g) daikon radish, cut into thin
   strips
3/4 cup (115 g) finely sliced cucumber
1/2 cup (50 g) finely sliced beetroot
1/2 avocado, cut into thin strips
2 dried black Chinese mushrooms, soaked to
   soften, stems discarded, caps thinly sliced
1 1/4 oz (40 g) dried glass noodles (*tang hoon*),
   soaked in warm water to soften, drained
   and cut into short lengths
1/2 cup (20 g) mint leaves
1/2 cup (20 g) fresh coriander leaves (cilantro)
1 green onion (scallion), cut into short lengths
1 red finger-length chili, deseeded and finely
   sliced lengthwise
4 dried rice paper wrappers (8 in/20 cm in
   diameter)
Fish Sauce Dip (page 27), to serve
Tamarind Avocado Dip (page 27), to serve
Fragrant Sweet Soy Sambal (page 25), to
   serve

PICKLED BEAN SPROUTS
1/2 cup (125 ml) water
1/4 cup (60 ml) white vinegar
1/4 cup (50 g) sugar
1/2 teaspoon salt
1 1/2 cups (75 g) fresh bean sprouts, coats and
   tails discarded

Makes 4 rolls
Preparation time: 25 mins + refrigerating time
Cooking time: 10 mins

Fresh summer rolls

Don't be intimidated by the long list of ingredients in this recipe.
The tangy accompaniments to these fresh-flavored rolls can be
prepared well in advance. Shortly before serving, prepare the vegetables
and wrap them in softened dried rice paper wrappers.

1 To prepare the Pickled Bean Sprouts, put the water, vinegar, sugar and salt in a small
saucepan and bring to a boil, stirring until the sugar completely dissolves. Allow to cool, then
pour over the bean sprouts. Refrigerate for 1 hour before serving.

2 Just before serving, arrange all the prepared vegetables and herbs on a clean work surface.
Dip a dried rice paper wrapper in a bowl of warm water for a few seconds until it starts to
soften. Remove and place on a clean damp kitchen cloth. Smooth the rice paper with your
fingers. Repeat with a second dried rice paper wrapper.

3 Neatly arrange one-quarter of each of the vegetables, noodles and herbs end-to-end across
the center of the rice paper, to within 3/4 in (2 cm) of each side. Roll up the rice paper, tucking
in the edges to make a cigar that completely encloses the filling. Repeat with the remaining
rice papers. Cut each roll into 4–5 bite-sized portions and transfer to a serving plate. Add one-
quarter of the Pickled Bean Sprouts and sprinkle over some of the sliced red chili. Serve with 1
or all 3 following dips: Fish Sauce Dip, Tamarind Avocado Dip and Fragrant Sweet Soy Sambal
in separate sauce bowls.

soups and salads

14 oz (400 g) fine fresh egg noodles, or 7 oz (200 g) dried noodles, cooked, rinsed and drained
1½ tablespoons oyster sauce
1½ tablespoons sesame oil
2½ cups (125 g) *choy sum* (Chinese greens), blanched
6 dried black Chinese mushrooms, soaked to soften, caps sliced
1 cup (200 g) shredded cooked chicken
4 cups (1 liter) chicken stock
1 tablespoon preserved Chinese cabbage (*tang chye*), optional
2 tablespoons finely sliced green onions (scallions)
4 teaspoons Crispy Fried Shallots (page 31)
Crispy Fried Wontons (page 40), as accompaniment
1 portion Sweet Chili Sauce (page 26), for dipping

Chicken noodle soup

Vendors pushing carts along Asian streets, stopping to sell bowls of noodle soup, were once a common sight. Even though some of the mobile vendors are disappearing, really good noodle soups such as this—flavored with chicken, mushrooms, and vegetable and served with Crispy Fried Wontons (see page 40)—can still be enjoyed at home.

1 Put the drained noodles in a bowl. Toss with the oyster sauce and sesame oil. Divide the noodles between 4 bowls. Add some of the *choy sum*, mushrooms and shredded chicken.
2 Bring the chicken stock to a boil. Ladle the hot stock into each bowl of noodles. Top the noodles with some of the preserved Chinese cabbage, green onions and Crispy Fried Shallots. Serve accompanied by Crispy Fried Wontons and a small bowl of Sweet Chili Sauce for dipping.

Serves 4   Preparation time: 15 mins   Cooking time: 25 mins

Sweet corn and leek soup with crab dumplings

This elegant, creamy soup is made with leek, sweet corn, celery and chicken stock, and is served with tiny dumplings of crabmeat mixed with chicken and perfumed with cilantro. With its subtle yet satisfying flavors, it makes a perfect start to any meal.

¼ cup (½ stick/60g) unsalted butter
1 small onion, sliced
4–5 cloves garlic, minced
½ stalk celery, sliced
3½ cups (250 g) white portion of leek, thinly sliced
2 cups (250 g) fresh or canned corn kernels
1 bay leaf
4 cups (1 liter) chicken stock
Salt and pepper, to taste
1 tomato, diced, to garnish
1 green onion (scallion), finely sliced, to garnish
Bread sticks, to garnish

CRAB DUMPLINGS
1 cup (120 g) cooked crabmeat
½ cup (100 g) ground chicken
1 clove garlic, minced
1 tablespoon finely chopped fresh coriander leaves (cilantro)
¼ teaspoon ground coriander
3 tablespoons heavy cream
¼ teaspoon salt
Liberal sprinkling of ground white pepper
16 wonton wrappers
2 teaspoons cornstarch

1 Heat the butter in a large saucepan. Stir-fry the onion and garlic over low-medium heat until transparent, about 3 minutes. Add the celery, leek and corn kernels. Stir-fry until softened, about 4 minutes. Add the bay leaf and chicken stock. Bring to a boil and season with salt and pepper. Cover, lower the heat, and simmer until the vegetables are soft, 20–25 minutes.

2 Make the Crab Dumplings by combining the crabmeat, ground chicken, garlic, coriander leaves, ground coriander, cream, salt and pepper in a food processor and pulse several times to mix well. Moisten the edges of a wonton wrapper with water. Put 1 heaping teaspoon of the crabmeat mixture in the center. Lift up the sides to enclose the filling and pinch the wrapper together to seal. Sprinkle a plate with the cornstarch and put the dumplings on top. Repeat with the remaining filling and wrappers to make more dumplings.

3 Bring a large pan of water to a boil. Add the dumplings, a few at a time and simmer gently until they rise to the surface and are cooked, about 3 minutes. Drain.

4 Reheat the soup gently and then ladle into four bowls and add four dumplings to each bowl. Garnish with tomato cubes, green onions and bread sticks. Serve hot.

Serves 4   Preparation time: 15 mins   Cooking time: 50 mins

1½ cups (375 ml) fresh carrot juice
16 fresh shrimp, peeled and deveined, tail
    section left intact
4 stalks lemongrass, tender inner part of
    bottom third only, finely sliced
1–2 red finger-length chilies, deseeded and
    finely sliced
1 tablespoon finely chopped fresh coriander
    leaves (cilantro)
1 tablespoon finely chopped mint leaves
4 kaffir lime leaves, finely sliced
4 baby carrots, blanched
4 baby turnips, blanched
8 fresh asparagus spears, sliced and blanched
1 small zucchini, sliced and blanched
2 tablespoons fish sauce, or more to taste
1 tablespoon fresh lime juice, or more to taste
Salt and ground black pepper, to taste
½ cup (1 stick/125 g) unsalted butter
Sprigs of fresh coriander leaves (cilantro), to
    garnish

Tropical carrot soup with shrimp

This inspired combination of tropical Asian flavors—lemongrass, coriander leaves, chilies, fish sauce and lime juice with shrimp, fresh carrot juice and baby vegetables is not only full of flavor and nutrition, but is so attractive that it can be served on any occasion. The cooking broth is enriched with butter, making this a sophisticated example of East meeting West.

1 Put the carrot juice in a saucepan and add the shrimp, lemongrass, chilies, coriander leaves, mint and kaffir lime leaves. Bring to a boil, stirring once or twice, then add the vegetables and simmer until the shrimp are just cooked, about 3 minutes. Do not overcook.

2 Season to taste with the fish sauce, lime juice, salt and pepper. Remove the shrimp and vegetables with a slotted spoon and place in a bowl. Add the butter to the liquid in the pan and cook over low heat, whisking constantly, until the butter is absorbed. Pour over the shrimp and vegetables, garnish with sprigs of coriander leaves and serve immediately.

Serves 4   Preparation time: 10 mins   Cooking time: 5 mins

Tomato and lentil soup

This pleasant, mild soup has definite Indian overtones, although soup is rarely part of a meal in India. A mixture of yellow and red lentils and tomatoes are simmered in freshly made vegetable stock, lightly flavored with spices and herbs. This is an ideal starter to any meal, or is good as part of a light lunch if served with Indian or French bread, followed by a salad.

³/₄ cup (125 g) yellow lentils, washed and drained
³/₄ cup (125 g) red lentils, washed and drain
One 16 oz (450 g) can peeled chopped tomatoes
Salt and ground black pepper, to taste
Oil, for deep-frying
4 slices curd cheese (*paneer*) or baked ricotta
Crispy fried curry leaves, to garnish
Fresh coriander leaves (cilantro), to garnish

VEGETABLE STOCK
1 small carrot, diced
½ onion, sliced
1 white part of a leek, sliced
1 stalk celery, sliced
1 teaspoon whole black peppercorns
2 whole cloves
1 short cinnamon stick
¹/₃ cup (15 g) chopped fresh coriander leaves (cilantro) and stems
¹/₄ cup (10 g) chopped mint leaves and stems
4 cups (1 liter) water
½ teaspoon salt

NOTE: A good alternative to the deep-fried curd cheese is 1 tablespoon thick sour cream with a sprinkle of ground cumin and a sprig of fresh coriander leaves on top of each bowl of soup.

1 To prepare the Vegetable Stock, put all the ingredients in a pot. Bring to a boil, cover, lower the heat and simmer for 45 minutes. Strain, pressing down with a wooden spoon to squeeze all the liquid from the vegetables. Discard the solids.

2 Rinse the pot and return the stock to it together with the lentils. Bring to a boil, cover, lower the heat and simmer until the lentils are very soft, about 15 minutes.

3 Add the tomatoes and cook until very soft, 10–12 minutes. Process in a blender until smooth then strain the soup through a fine sieve. Add salt and pepper to taste.

4 Heat the oil in a small pan and deep-fry the sliced *paneer* until golden brown. Drain on paper towels. Transfer the soup to 4 serving bowls, add a slice of *paneer* to each bowl and garnish with the crispy fried curry leaves and fresh coriander leaves.

Serves 4   Preparation time: 20 mins   Cooking time: 1 hour + 20 mins

Spicy beef soup

This satisfying soup is inspired by the hot, fragrant Soto Padang from the west coast of the island of Sumatra in Indonesia. The beef stock is simmered with an aromatic spice paste, sour tamarind and a touch of palm sugar, then strained and served with paper-thin slices of seared beef, crunchy bean sprouts, daikon radish and Crispy Fried Shallots. Serve with steamed rice and a mixed vegetable dish makes it a complete and healthy meal.

10 oz (300 g) tender beef, seared with a little oil in a pan and then thinly sliced

8–12 thin slices daikon radish or potato, blanched, to garnish

1 small carrot, thinly sliced, blanched, to garnish

4 kaffir lime leaves, finely sliced, to garnish

4 teaspoons Crispy Fried Shallots (page 31), to garnish

1 cup (50 g) fresh bean sprouts, washed and drained, coats and tails discarded, to garnish

1 green onion (scallion), finely sliced, to garnish

STOCK

5 cups (1.25 liters) beef stock, preferably freshly made

2 stalks lemongrass, tender inner part of bottom third only, bruised and cut into short lengths

2 teaspoons shaved palm sugar or dark brown sugar

1 tablespoon tamarind pulp

Salt and ground white pepper, to taste

SPICE PASTE

5 small shallots, sliced

4–6 cloves garlic, sliced

2 in (5 cm) galangal root, sliced

½ in (12 mm) turmeric root, sliced or ½ teaspoon ground turmeric

½ teaspoon dried shrimp paste (belachan)

1–2 red finger-length chilies, sliced

4 candlenuts or macadamia nuts

2 tablespoons oil

1 To make the Spice Paste, process all the ingredients except the oil in a mortar or blender. Add a little of the oil, if necessary, to keep the mixture turning. Heat the remaining oil in a pot and add the ground mixture. Stir-fry over low heat until fragrant, 4–5 minutes.

2 Add all the Stock ingredients to the pot and bring to a boil, stirring frequently. Cover, lower the heat and simmer for 45 minutes. Strain the Stock through a sieve, pressing down with the back of a spoon to extract all the liquid. Discard the solids and return the stock to the pot.

3 Reheat the soup, taste and add salt and pepper if required. Divide into 4 soup bowls. Top each bowl with a few slices of the beef and add a little of each of the garnishes. Serve hot.

NOTE: To slice kaffir lime leaves quickly and easily, roll up firmly, from stem to tip end rather than side to side. Place on a cutting board and slice very finely with a sharp knife, discarding the central rib.

Serves 4   Preparation time: 20 mins   Cooking time: 1 hour

4 cups (1 liter) water
1 teaspoon salt
1 teaspoon sugar
2 cups (500 ml) coconut milk
1¼ lbs (600 g) fresh laksa rice noodles,
    blanched in hot water for 30 seconds and
    drained or 10 oz (300 g) dried rice stick
    noodles, blanched and drained
1½ cups (75 g) fresh bean sprouts
4 hard-boiled eggs, quartered
12 fresh scallops, blanched until cooked
12 cooked shrimp, peeled and deveined
4 pieces deep-fried tofu, blanched for 30
    seconds, sliced and drained
1 portion Chili Sambal with Lime (page 25)

LAKSA PASTE
3 small onions, sliced
2 in (5 cm) galangal root, sliced
6 cloves garlic, minced
3 in (7.5 cm) fresh ginger root, sliced
3 stalks lemongrass, tender inner part of
    bottom third only, sliced
4–5 red finger-length chilies, deseeded and
    sliced
¼ cup (60 ml) oil
2–3 teaspoons ground red pepper (cayenne)
2 teaspoons ground turmeric
3 teaspoons ground coriander
¾ cup (40 g) laksa leaves (Vietnamese mint or
    polygonum)
2 teaspoons dried shrimp paste (*belachan*)
¾ cup (90 g) dried shrimp, soaked in water to
    soften, drained and then ground to a fine
    powder in a blender

Singapore seafood laksa

This sophisticated Singapore laksa contains scallops and shrimp as well as the usual bean sprouts, deep-fried tofu and a spicy hot coconut milk broth bathing fresh rice noodles. Although often eaten as a hearty breakfast in Asia, this laksa is just as good for lunch.

1 Make the Laksa Paste by processing the onion, galangal, garlic, ginger, lemongrass and chilies to a paste. Heat the oil in a wok, add the spice paste and stir-fry over low-medium heat until the moisture has dried up and the oil starts to separate, about 10 minutes. Add the ground red pepper, ground turmeric, coriander and laksa leaves, and stir-fry for 1 minute. Add the dried shrimp paste and stir-fry for 1 more minute, then add the ground dried shrimp and stir-fry for 1 minute. Transfer the Laksa Paste to a bowl and leave to cool.

2 To make the gravy, heat a large pot and add the Laksa Paste then stir in the water, salt and sugar. Bring to a boil, lower the heat and simmer uncovered for 10 minutes. Add the coconut milk and bring almost to a boil, then quickly remove from the heat.

3 To serve, divide the drained noodles into 4 large serving bowls. Fill each bowl with some of the hot gravy, then add the bean sprouts, egg, scallops, shrimp and tofu slices to each bowl. Serve with the Chili Sambal with Lime.

Serves 4   Preparation time: 20 mins   Cooking time: 35 mins

Sumatran chicken laksa

Laksa, a noodle soup with spicy coconut milk broth and rice noodles, is popular in Malaysia, Singapore and Indonesia. Chicken, bean sprouts, tofu and boiled eggs enrich this satisfying Sumatran version, which relies on freshly made laksa paste for maximum flavor.

2 tablespoons oil
3 cups (750 ml) coconut milk
3 cups (750 ml) chicken stock
2 cups (14 oz/400 g) shredded cooked chicken
   breast or thigh
Salt and black pepper, to taste
1¼ lbs (600 g) fresh or 10 oz (300 g) dried
   rice stick noodles, cooked in boiling water,
   drained
1½ cups (75 g) fresh bean sprouts, coats and
   tails discarded
2 hard-boiled eggs, sliced
1 cake (10 oz/300 g) fried tofu, sliced
2 tablespoons chopped fresh coriander leaves
   (cilantro)
2 tablespoons sliced green onions (scallions)
1 red finger-length chili, deseeded and sliced
1 lime or lemon, quartered
1 portion Chili Sambal with Lime (page 25)

LAKSA PASTE
2 tablespoons small dried shrimp, soaked in
   hot water to soften, drained
8 small shallots, sliced
4–5 cloves garlic, sliced
2 in (5 cm) galangal root, sliced
2 in (5 cm) turmeric root, sliced or 2
   teaspoons ground turmeric
6 candlenuts or macadamia nuts
5–6 red finger-length chilies, sliced
2 stalks lemongrass, tender inner part of
   bottom third only, sliced
1½ teaspoons dried shrimp paste (*belachan*),
   dry-roasted
3 teaspoons fish sauce
½ cup (125 ml) coconut cream

1 Make the Laksa Paste by processing the dried shrimp in a blender until finely shredded. Add the remaining ingredients except the coconut cream and process until coarsely ground. Add the coconut cream and process to a paste.

2 Heat the oil in a large saucepan and add the Laksa Paste. Stir-fry over low-medium heat until fragrant, 4–5 minutes. Slowly add the coconut milk, stir to mix well, then add the chicken stock. Bring to a boil, lower the heat and simmer uncovered, 10 minutes. Add the cooked chicken breast and simmer for 1 minute. Taste and add salt and black pepper, if desired.

3 To serve, divide the noodles into 4 large serving bowls. Top with the gravy and garnish each serving with some of the bean sprouts, egg slices, tofu, coriander leaves, green onions and sliced chilies. Serve with lime wedges and Chili Sambal with Lime.

Serves 4   Preparation time: 20 mins   Cooking time: 35 mins

Tropical chicken salad

This Balinese classic begins with chicken seasoned with salt, garlic, and lemongrass. After roasting, the meat is shredded and mixed with green beans, chilies, kaffir lime leaves, lime juice, lemon basil and Shrimp Paste Sambal (page 24) to make a tangy, fragrant treat. Both the chicken and the sambal can be prepared in advance and combined at the last minute.

1 fresh chicken, about 2½ lbs (1¼ kg), cut in half, skin discarded
1 stalk lemongrass, tender inner part of bottom third only, sliced
4 cloves garlic
1 teaspoon salt
¼ teaspoon ground black pepper
2 tablespoons oil
1 portion Shrimp Paste Sambal (page 24)
2 cups (200 g) diagonally sliced green beans, blanched until cooked but still firm, drained and plunged in ice-cold water, then drained again
1 tablespoon fresh lime juice
1–2 red finger-length chilies, deseeded and finely sliced
3 kaffir lime leaves, finely sliced
½ cup (20 g) lemon basil leaves
Lime wedges, to serve

1 Preheat the oven to 350°F (180°C).

2 Prick the chicken all over with a fork to allow the marinade to penetrate. Process the lemongrass, garlic, salt and pepper to a fine paste in a mortar or blender, adding a little oil to keep the blades turning. Transfer the mixture to a bowl and stir in the remaining oil. Coat the chicken all over with the paste, place on a baking dish and cook in the preheated oven for 45 minutes. Allow to cool and shred the meat into strips. Set aside.

3 Just before serving, place the chicken in a large bowl and add the Shrimp Paste Sambal. Toss to mix well then add the green beans, lime juice, chilies, kaffir lime leaves and basil leaves. Toss again. Taste and add salt and black pepper if desired. Serve with lime wedges on the side.

Serves 4   Preparation time: 15 mins
Cooking time: 45 mins

10 oz (300 g) fresh skinned and boneless
   mackerel or herring fillets
1 cup (150 g) daikon radish, sliced into
   matchsticks
2 cups (300 g) cucumber, core removed, sliced
   into matchsticks
1 red finger-length chili, deseeded and finely
   sliced lengthwise
3/4 in (2 cm) fresh ginger root, thinly sliced
4 baby pickled onions (optional)
4 sprigs fresh coriander leaves (cilantro)
1 tablespoon sliced green onions (scallions)
1 tablespoon finely chopped chervil or parsley
2 teaspoons sesame seeds, roasted until
   golden brown
2 tablespoons salmon roe

SOY LIME DRESSING
2 tablespoons lime or lemon juice
1 tablespoon soy sauce
2 teaspoons Shallot Oil (page 31)
2 teaspoons sesame oil
2 teaspoons rice wine or sake
2 teaspoons sugar
½ teaspoon salt
Liberal sprinkling of ground white pepper

Sashimi salad with soy lime dressing

Dishes where fresh fish is "cooked" with a dressing or marinade of lime juice are common throughout tropical Asia. Chinese in Singapore enjoy raw fish salad during the annual Lunar New Year celebrations and their classic recipe has inspired this modern interpretation. Tangy, fragrant and with contrasting textures, this makes an ideal starter or light lunch.

1 Chill the fish in the freezer for 10–15 minutes to firm. Cut into thin slices.
2 Prepare the Soy Lime Dressing by combining and whisking all the ingredients together in a small bowl.
3 Arrange the daikon, cucumber, chili, ginger, pickled onions (if using) and coriander leaves and stems on a serving plate, then top with slices of fish and sprinkle with the green onions, chervil or parsley and sesame seeds. Garnish with the salmon roe and drizzle with the Soy Lime Dressing.

Serves 4   Preparation time: 15 mins + chilling time

2 green apples or water apples or 1 starfruit, cut into wedges

1 cup (160 g) firm ripe papaya, peeled and cut into chunks

³/₄ cup (150 g) fresh pineapple, peeled and cut into chunks

1½ cups (150 g) jicama (*bangkuang*), or 1 *salak* (snake fruit), peeled and cut into chunks

1 unripe green mango, peeled, pitted and sliced

SPICY PALM SUGAR DRESSING
4 tablespoons tamarind pulp
½ cup (90 g) shaved palm sugar or dark brown sugar
³/₄ cup (180 ml) water
½ teaspoon salt
2–3 bird's-eye chilies, deseeded and sliced
1 teaspoon dried shrimp paste (*belachan*), dry-roasted

Serves 4
Preparation time: 15 mins
Cooking time: 15 mins

Tropical fruit salad (rujak) with spicy palm sugar dressing

Little distinction is made between fruits and vegetables in the tropics, with avocadoes eaten with sugar or cream and pineapple eaten with salt or hot spicy dips. In Indonesia, Malaysia and Singapore, a mixture of refreshing fruits and crunchy vegetables is tossed with a tamarind and palm sugar syrup accented with chili and dried shrimp paste to make a delightfully different salad, known locally as *rujak*.

1 To make the Spicy Palm Sugar Dressing, combine the tamarind, sugar, water and salt in a small saucepan. Bring to a boil, stirring until the sugar dissolves. Lower the heat and simmer uncovered until the mixture thickens and turns syrupy, 12–15 minutes. Strain into a bowl, pressing the pulp to obtain as much juice as possible. Discard the solids. Pound the salt, chilies and dried shrimp paste to form a paste. Stir this in to the syrup and allow to cool before using.

2 Just before serving, combine the water apple, papaya, pineapple, jicama and mango in a bowl. Pour over the Spicy Palm Sugar Dressing and toss to mix well.

Simple tamarind dressing salad

Known in India as ketchumbar, this salad is normally served as a side dish with rice, meat and cooked vegetables or lentils, but can also be enjoyed as an appetizer. This salad makes an excellent accompaniment to Shrimp Biryani Rice (page 75).

1 cucumber, sliced into matchsticks
1 carrot, sliced into matchsticks
½ beetroot, sliced into matchsticks
1 tomato, deseeded and finely sliced
1 bell pepper, finely sliced
1 small onion, halved and thinly sliced
½ cup (20 g) chopped fresh coriander leaves
   (cilantro)
2 tablespoons lime or lemon juice
1 tablespoon tamarind pulp, soaked in 3
   tablespoons warm water, mashed and
   strained to obtain the juice
½ teaspoon salt

Place all the vegetables, onion and coriander leaves in a bowl. Sprinkle the lime juice and tamarind juice over the salad. Add the salt and toss again. Chill before serving.

Serves 4   Preparation time: 10 mins

1 fresh banana bud, or one 14-oz (400-g) can
   heart of palm
½ small onion, thinly sliced
6 cherry tomatoes, halved, or 1 small tomato,
   cut into small wedges
1 stalk lemongrass, tender inner part of
   bottom third only, thinly sliced
1 fresh lime, cut into wedges
1 small cucumber, finely sliced
1 starfruit, thinly sliced
Few sprigs of basil (optional)

SPICY COCONUT DRESSING
2 small shallots, sliced
1 red finger-length chili, sliced
2 stalks lemongrass, tender inner part of
   bottom third only, sliced
1 tablespoon oil
½ teaspoon dried shrimp paste (*belachan*),
   dry-roasted
1 tablespoon curry powder
¾ cup (180 ml) coconut milk
6 oz (180 g) fresh shrimp, peeled and
   deveined
1 teaspoon fresh lime juice
1 teaspoon sugar
½ teaspoon salt

Serves 4
Preparation time: 15 mins + soaking time
Cooking time: 35 mins

Tropical shrimp salad

This exotic salad is a modern interpretation of a Nonya classic. In this recipe, a spicy coconut milk dressing is poured over a salad of raw fruit and vegetables, cooked shrimp and tender strips of banana bud, all served in banana petals.

1 Remove the reddish outside petals of the banana bud and set aside for serving. Peel and discard the remaining outer leaves until you get to the paler colored tender inner portion. Put the banana bud in a large bowl of salted water with a weight on top. Soak for 4 hours, or overnight. Drain.

2 Bring a large saucepan of lightly salted water to a boil and add the banana bud. Simmer until tender when tested with a skewer, about 20 minutes. Drain, cool, then cut in half lengthwise. Cut across in thin slices, pulling away any strands of sap and pinching the tips of the long enclosed flowers to remove and discard the hard filament inside.

3 Make the Spicy Coconut Dressing by processing the shallots, chili and lemongrass to a paste in a mortar or blender. Heat the oil in a saucepan and stir-fry the spice paste over medium heat until fragrant, 3 minutes. Add the dried shrimp paste and curry powder and stir-fry for about 30 seconds. Slowly pour in the coconut milk and bring to a boil, stirring. Reduce the heat and simmer until the liquid has reduced slightly, 3–4 minutes. Add the shrimp, lime juice, sugar and salt, and cook uncovered, stirring frequently, until the shrimp are just cooked, about 3 minutes.

4 Remove the shrimp from the Spicy Coconut Dressing. Divide the shrimp, sliced softened banana buds, onion, tomatoes, lemongrass, lime, cucumber and starfruit into 4 large banana petals (or serving dishes). Pour over the dressing and garnish with sprigs of basil, if desired.

Green mango salad

This popular Thai salad is bursting with bright tart flavor and a nice mix of textures. Unripe tart green mangoes are typically available in Asian and Indian markets.

3 unripe green mangoes, finely sliced to yield about 2 cups (240 g) flesh
1–2 red finger-length chilies, deseeded and finely sliced
1 tablespoon finely chopped fresh coriander leaves (cilantro)
1 tablespoon finely chopped mint leaves
1 tablespoon fresh lime juice
1 tablespoon shaved palm sugar or brown sugar
1½ teaspoons fish sauce
4–6 small dried shrimp, processed to a powder

Combine all the ingredients and mix well. Refrigerate the salad in a covered container until ready to serve.

NOTE: If you cannot find green mangoes, simply buy the least ripe mangoes that you can find and double the amount of lime juice added.

Serves 4   Preparation time: 10 mins

Fennel and pumpkin slaw

This hearty slaw is tossed with an aromatic Lime Chili Dressing. The flavor of fennel and pumpkin make it a perfect side dish for Barbecued Baby Back Spareribs (page 93).

1 red finger-length chili, deseeded and finely sliced
³/₄ cup (75 g) finely shredded Chinese (Napa) cabbage
³/₄ cup (80 g) finely sliced fennel
½ cup (80 g) finely sliced pumpkin
1 green onion (scallion), sliced

LIME CHILI DRESSING
2 tablespoons water
4 teaspoons sugar
2 tablespoons fish sauce
3 tablespoons fresh lime juice
2 stalks lemongrass, tender inner part of bottom third only, finely sliced
1 kaffir lime leaf, finely sliced
2–3 small shallots, finely sliced
1 red bird's-eye chili, deseeded and finely sliced
2 teaspoons finely chopped mint
2 teaspoons finely chopped coriander leaves (cilantro)

1 Make the Lime Chili Dressing by putting the water and sugar in a small saucepan and bring to a boil, stirring. Simmer until the mixture thickens a little, then transfer to a bowl to cool. Stir in all the other ingredients. Taste and add extra lime juice or fish sauce if required.
2 Combine the chili, shredded cabbage, finely sliced fennel and pumpkin, and sliced green onions in a bowl. Toss to mix, then add the Lime Chili Dressing and toss again. Refrigerate until ready to serve.

Serves 4   Preparation time: 10 mins   Cooking time: 10 mins

rice, noodles and bread

Hainanese chicken rice

A Hainanese classic that is one of Singapore's most popular dishes, chicken rice has several components: poached chicken; rice cooked with a touch of chicken fat; Chili Sauce, thick dark soy sauce and Ginger Sauce for adding to taste. In this recipe, the rice is flavored with fragrant pandanus leaves—a distinctly Tropical touch.

1 large chicken
10½ cups (2.5 liters) water
3 cloves garlic, peeled
2 slices fresh ginger root
Sesame oil, for rubbing
Thick dark soy sauce, fresh sprigs of coriander leaves (cilantro), cucumber slices, green onions (scallions), to serve

RICE
3 cups (600 g) uncooked rice
2 tablespoons minced garlic
1½ tablespoons minced fresh ginger root
1 tablespoon finely chopped shallots
2 pandanus leaves, tied into a knot
2 teaspoons salt, or to taste

CHILI SAUCE
6 red finger-length chilies
3–5 bird's-eye chilies
2 cloves garlic
2 teaspoons minced fresh ginger root
½ teaspoon sugar
½ teaspoon salt, or to taste
2 tablespoons kalamansi lime juice

GINGER SAUCE
100 g (3½ oz) fresh old ginger root, peeled and sliced
1 tablespoon oil

1 Clean the chicken thoroughly. Remove the excess fat and reserve. Bring the water to a rolling boil in a large, deep pot. Fully submerge the chicken in the boiling water. Return to a rolling boil. Simmer vigorously, partially covered, for 15 minutes, then cover tightly, switch off the heat and let stand for 20 minutes.

2 Remove the chicken from the hot stock. Rub the chicken skin with the sesame oil and set aside.

3 To prepare the Rice, wash the rice grains well and drain, then spread out on a large plate and let it dry, 10–15 minutes. Chop the reserved chicken fat into small pieces. Combine with 2 tablespoons cold water in a small pot and cook over low heat for 10–15 minutes, until the water has evaporated and fat has rendered.

4 Heat 5 tablespoons of the rendered chicken fat in a wok over medium heat. Fry the garlic, ginger and shallots until fragrant, 1–2 minutes. Add the rice and stir-fry gently for 2–3 minutes or until the grains turn translucent. Transfer the rice to a rice cooker, add the pandanus leaves, salt and 3 cups (750 ml) of the stock from the chicken pot. Switch on and leave to cook. Discard the pandanus leaves before serving.

5 To make the Chilli Sauce, blend all the ingredients to form a paste, then add 2 tablespoons hot stock and blend until combined.

6 To make the Ginger Sauce, blend the ginger to a paste, then add the oil and 1 tablespoon of the hot chicken stock and blend until combined.

7 Chop the chicken into pieces and placed them on the bed of cucumber slices. Garnish with coriander leaves and green onions before serving with the rice, dipping bowls of Chili Sauce, Ginger Sauce and thick dark soy sauce.

Serves 4–6   Preparation time: 45 mins   Cooking time: 30 mins

3 tablespoons oil
4 eggs, lightly beaten
4 cloves garlic, minced
1¼ lbs (600 g) fresh egg noodles or pasta
7 oz (200 g) fresh rice noodles (see note)
1½ cups (75 g) fresh bean sprouts
5 oz (150 g) Japanese or Chinese fish cake, sliced (optional)
16–20 small cooked shrimp, peeled and deveined
5 oz (150 g) cooked squid, sliced
5 oz (150 g) cooked pork, sliced
Salt and ground white pepper to taste
½ cup (20 g) sliced Chinese chives (*gu cai*), in short lengths
1 portion Sambal Belachan (page 24), to serve
2 red finger-length chilies, deseeded and sliced, to serve
4 small limes (kalamansi) cut in half, or 1 large lime, quartered, to serve

PORK STOCK
2 lbs (1 kg) chicken bones for stock, blanched in boiling water for 3 minutes
2 lbs (1 kg) pork bones, blanched in boiling water for 3 minutes
6 cups (1.4 liters) water
3 in (7.5 cm) fresh ginger root, bruised
3 cloves garlic, smashed
1½ teaspoons salt

NOTE: If you do not have a very large wok, you may need to cook the noodles in two separate batches. If you cannot obtain fresh noodles, use ½ the quantity called for of dry noodles and blanch them quickly, then drain.

Hokkien noodles

Hokkien mee (noodles), as this dish is known in Singapore, originated in southern China, in Fujian province. A mixture of yellow noodles and rice flour noodles is stir-fried with eggs, bean sprouts, chives, seafood and pork, then simmered in concentrated pork stock. A distinctly local touch comes in the form of the accompanying Sambal Belachan, a pungent paste of chilies, shallots, dried shrimp paste and lime. This hearty noodle dish can be enjoyed any time of the day or night.

1 Prepare the Pork Stock by placing all the ingredients in a pot. Bring to a boil, cover, reduce the heat and simmer for 2 hours. Strain, discarding the bones, then boil the strained stock, pot uncovered if necessary, to reduce the stock to 2 cups (500 ml). Set aside.
2 Heat half of the oil in a large wok until very hot. Add the egg and stir-fry until it just starts to set, then add the remaining oil and the garlic and stir-fry for 10 seconds. Add both lots of noodles, bean sprouts, fish cake, shrimp, squid and pork and stir-fry for 1–2 minutes, using two wok spatulas to mix the ingredients thoroughly.
3 Add 2 cups (500 ml) prepared Pork Stock and stir until the liquid is almost dried up. Season with salt and pepper and transfer to a serving dish. Garnish with the Chinese chives and serve accompanied by the Sambal Belachan, sliced chilies and lime.

Serves 4   Preparation time: 15 mins   Cooking time: 2 hours 40 mins

Coconut rice with assorted side dishes

This version of nasi campur (literally "mixed rice") is like a mini-Rijsttafel with pandanus-flavored coconut rice; Chicken with Sweet Soy and Chili Sauce; Shrimp Crackers with Crispy Eggs; Balinese Mixed Vegetables (page 121); Pickled Cucumber (page 31); Crispy Tempeh (page 121) and Sweet Palm Sugar Sambal (page 25). Several of the components can be prepared well in advance. You can also prepare any of these recipes individually to serve with plain rice and other dishes.

1 portion Chicken with Sweet Soy and Chili
  Sauce (page 87)
1 portion Balinese Mixed Vegetables (page
  121)
1 portion Crispy Tempeh (page 121)
1 portion Pickled Cucumber (page 31)

COCONUT RICE
4 cloves garlic, smashed
1 pandanus leaf, raked with a fork and tied in
  a knot
1 kaffir lime leaf, edges torn
1 *salam* leaf (optional)
½ teaspoon salt
1 cup (250 ml) coconut milk
1½ cups (375 ml) water
2 cups (400 g) uncooked long-grain rice,
  washed and drained

SHRIMP CRACKERS WITH CRISPY EGGS
8 dried crackers (*krupuk*), dried in the sun or
  in the oven on very low heat
Oil, for deep-frying
4 hard-boiled eggs, peeled
1 portion Sweet Palm Sugar Sambal (page 25),
  to serve

1 To make the Coconut Rice, put all the ingredients except the rice in a saucepan with a heavy base and bring slowly to a boil, stirring frequently.

2 Add the rice, stir, then partially cover the pan with a lid. Cook over medium heat until the coconut milk is completely absorbed and "craters" form on the surface, about 5 minutes. Cover the pan firmly, turn off the heat and stand for 5 minutes. Wipe the inside of the lid with a towel, cover the pan firmly and cook over very low heat, about 15 minutes. Remove from the heat.

3 Remove the 3 kinds of leaves, and fluff up the rice with a fork. Cover and stand for at least 5 minutes, or up to 20 minutes before serving.

4 To make the Shrimp Crackers with Crispy Eggs, heat the oil in a large pan and add a few crackers at a time. When they expand, remove with a slotted spoon and drain.

5 Deep-fry the hard-boiled eggs until crisp and golden brown on the outside. Drain on paper towels, cut in half and serve with the Sweet Palm Sugar Sambal.

Serves 4–6   Preparation time: 20 mins   Cooking time: 1 hour

Shrimp biryani rice

Biryani is a festive Indian dish which requires three separate stages of preparation: cooking a spicy curry, preparing a fragrant pilau-style rice and combining the rice and shrimp to finish the biryani in the oven. Serve with the Simple Tamarind Dressing Salad (page 65).

1¼ lbs (600 g) fresh shrimp
2 tablespoons oil
6 cardamom pods, slit and bruised
3 whole cloves
1 teaspoon cumin seeds
1 long cinnamon stick
2 tej patta (Indian dried bay leaves) or regular
   bay leaves
10 black peppercorns
2 small onions, thinly sliced
2 cloves garlic, minced
1 teaspoon minced fresh ginger root
2 teaspoons ground red pepper (cayenne)
2 teaspoons garam masala
1 teaspoon ground coriander
1 teaspoon ground cumin
3 ripe tomatoes, sliced
⅓ cup (80 ml) plain yogurt
2 tablespoons water
½ teaspoon salt
1 tablespoon finely chopped mint leaves
1 tablespoon finely chopped fresh coriander
   leaves (cilantro)

SHRIMP MARINADE
1 tablespoon minced garlic
2 teaspoons minced fresh ginger root
1 teaspoon salt
2 teaspoons fresh lime juice
1 teaspoon ground turmeric

BIRYANI RICE
Pinch saffron strands
1 tablespoon hot milk
1 tablespoon oil
4 cardamom pods, slit and bruised
2 whole cloves
1 teaspoon cumin seeds
2 tej patta (Indian dried bay leaves) or regular
   bay leaves
1 medium cinnamon stick
2¾ cups (680 ml) water
1 teaspoon salt
2 cups (400 g) uncooked Basmati rice, washed,
   soaked 30 minutes, then drained

GARNISHES
1½ tablespoons Crispy Fried Shallots
   (page 31)
1½ tablespoons cashew nuts, split in half
   lengthwise, fried in a little butter until
   golden
1½ tablespoons raisins, fried in a little butter
   until soft and swollen
1 tablespoon finely chopped mint leaves
Fresh coriander (cilantro) sprigs

1 Peel and devein the shrimp. Put them in a bowl.

2 Make the Shrimp Marinade by pounding or processing the garlic, ginger and salt to a paste, then stir in the lime juice and ground turmeric. Add to the shrimp and mix well. Set aside to marinate for 30 minutes.

3 To cook the marinated shrimp, heat the oil in a wok and add the cardamom, cloves, cumin seeds, cinnamon stick and tej patta (or bay leaves) and peppercorns. Stir-fry for 2–3 minutes, then add the onions and stir-fry until the onions start to brown, about 8 minutes. Add the garlic and ginger, stir-fry for 30 seconds, then add the ground red pepper, garam masala, ground coriander and cumin. Stir-fry for 1 minute, then add the tomatoes and cook until softened, 4–5 minutes. Add the marinated shrimp, yogurt, water and salt, stirring to mix well. Simmer uncovered until the shrimp are cooked, 4–5 minutes. Scatter the mint and coriander leaves on top.

4 To prepare the Biryani Rice, sprinkle the saffron on the hot milk and leave to soak for 15 minutes. Press on the strands to obtain maximum color, then set the milk and saffron aside. Heat the oil in a saucepan and add the cardamom, cloves, cumin, tej patta (or bay leaves) and cinnamon stick. Stir-fry for 2–3 minutes, then add the water and salt and bring to a boil. Add the drained rice, stir, then boil uncovered until the water has dried up and "craters" form on the surface, about 8 minutes. Sprinkle the saffron milk and strands over the rice, cover and reduce the heat to minimum. Cook for another 5 minutes. Fluff up the rice with a fork; set aside.

5 To complete the dish, preheat the oven to 350°F (180°C). Spread half the rice in the bottom of a large heatproof casserole dish with a firmly fitting lid. Spread the cooked shrimp on top, then cover the shrimp evenly with the remaining rice. Cover the dish and cook in the preheated oven for 12–15 minutes.

6 Garnish the biryani with the Crispy Fried Shallots, fried cashews, raisins, mint leaves and coriander sprigs. Serve, if desired, with plain yogurt or a Raita and Naan Bread (page 79) and Simple Tamarind Dressing Salad (page 65).

Serves 4–6   Preparation time: 20 mins + marinating time   Cooking time: 1 hour 20 mins

Fried egg noodles

Noodles are a favorite lunch or light meal throughout the region, with literally hundreds of different versions. This Indonesian-style dish of stir-fried egg noodles, known as *mee goreng* in Indonesia, is tasty and easily prepared, containing a mixture of shrimp, leafy greens, garlic, onions, carrot and chili, plus plenty of seasonings.

2 tablespoons oil
2 eggs, beaten
6–8 cloves garlic, chopped
14 oz (400 g) fresh shrimp, peeled and
   deveined, halved lengthwise
1 small onion, sliced into matchsticks
½ carrot, sliced into matchsticks
4 green onions (scallions), finely sliced
2 cups (100 g) chopped *choy sum* (Chinese
   greens) or Chinese (Napa) cabbage or other
   leafy greens
1 red finger-length chili, deseeded and sliced
1 lb (500 g) fresh egg noodles, blanched in
   boiling water and drained or 8 oz (250 g)
   dried egg noodles, blanched and drained
2 tablespoons Crispy Fried Shallots (page 31),
   to garnish

SAUCE
2 tablespoons sesame oil
2 tablespoons oyster sauce
2 teaspoons fish sauce
1 tablespoon thick sweet soy sauce
1 tablespoon bottled chili sauce
1 tablespoon rice wine (or sherry)

1 Make the Sauce by combining all the ingredients in a small bowl and set aside.

2 Prepare the omelet by heating a bit of oil in a skillet and frying the eggs in a thin layer until it sets. Remove from the pan and slice thinly on a cutting board. Set aside.

3 Heat the oil in a wok and add the garlic. Stir-fry for a few seconds, then add the shrimp and stir-fry over very high heat until they start to change color, about 30 seconds. Add the onion, carrot, green onion, *choy sum* or cabbage, and chilies. Stir-fry 2 more minutes. Pour in the Sauce, stirring to mix well. Add the noodles, tossing to mix well and heat through, about 1 minute. Transfer to a serving bowl and garnish with the omelet strips and Crispy Fried Shallots.

Serves 4   Preparation time: 10 mins
Cooking time: 15 mins

Vegetarian rice noodles

This meatless version of fried rice noodles has a light, refreshing flavor. Bean sprouts, carrot, meaty black Chinese mushrooms and green beans are stir-fried with garlic, onion and chilies, with fish sauce (or soy sauce, if you want to be strictly vegetarian), lime juice and chopped peanuts adding extra flavor and texture.

10 oz (300 g) dried rice stick noodles, blanched in hot water and drained
3 tablespoons oil
3 sprigs fresh Thai basil leaves
6–8 cloves garlic, finely chopped
4 eggs, lightly beaten
2 cups (100 g) fresh bean sprouts, washed and drained, straggly tails removed
1 small onion, halved lengthwise, thinly sliced
½ small carrot, finely sliced
4 dried black Chinese mushrooms, soaked in hot water for 15 minutes, drained, stems discarded, caps sliced
5–6 green beans, cut into short lengths
1–2 red finger-length chilies, deseeded and finely sliced
1 green onion (scallion), finely sliced
1 tablespoon ground red pepper (*cayenne*)
2 tablespoons sugar
⅓ cup (80 ml) fish sauce
⅓ cup (80 ml) fresh lime juice
3 tablespoons coarsely chopped dry roasted peanuts
Sprigs of fresh coriander leaves (cilantro), to garnish
1 lime or lemon, quartered

1 Blanch the noodles in boiling water then drain in a colander. Rinse under cold running water and drain again. Spread on a large plate.

2 Heat the oil in a wok and add the basil leaves. Fry quickly, then remove the leaves with a slotted spoon, drain on paper towels and set aside. Add the garlic to the wok and stir-fry over medium heat for a few seconds, then add the eggs and stir until they begin to set. Push the eggs to the sides, then add the bean sprouts, onion, carrot, mushrooms, beans, chili and green onion and stir-fry until the vegetables are almost cooked, about 2 minutes.

3 Add the noodles to the wok, add the ground red pepper, sugar, fish sauce and lime juice. Stir-fry to mix the noodles thoroughly with the other ingredients and heat through. Transfer to a serving dish. Garnish with the fried basil leaves, peanuts, coriander leaves and lime wedges.

Serves 4   Preparation time: 10 mins   Cooking time: 10 mins

Naan basket with chutneys & raita

An excellent dish to serve at parties, flavored naan is accompanied by a simple crudité of raw vegetables and fruit and a selection of chutneys and raita. Cooling yogurt-based Raita is a favorite accompaniment with spicy Indian food and can be served with curries and other spicy dishes.

1 portion Banana Chutney (page 29)
1 portion Green Chili Mango Chutney (page 30)

NAAN BREAD
³/₄ teaspoon superfine sugar
¹/₄ cup (50 ml) warm water
1 teaspoon instant yeast
2 cups (300 g) all-purpose (plain) flour
½ teaspoon salt
¹/₃ cup (80 ml) water
2 tablespoons plain yogurt
1 tablespoon melted butter

ACCOMPANIMENTS
Crudité of sliced raw vegetables and fruit such as coconut, cucumber, carrot, bell pepper
Lemon wedges

RAITA
¹/₃ cup (50 g) finely diced mixed vegetables, such as cucumber, small onion, carrot, tomato, green and red bell pepper
1 tablespoon finely chopped fresh coriander leaves (cilantro)
½ teaspoon ground cumin
½ teaspoon salt
½ cup (125 ml) thick plain yogurt, chilled

1 To make the Naan Bread, put the sugar and warm water in a bowl and sprinkle over the yeast. Leave in a warm place until it is dissolved and frothy, about 10 minutes.

2 Sift the flour and salt into a mixing bowl, then make a well in the center. Pour in the yeast mixture, water, yogurt and butter, stirring to make a soft dough. Add a little more flour if the dough seems sticky. Turn out and knead on a lightly floured surface for 10–15 minutes, until the dough is smooth and elastic. Lightly oil the mixing bowl, add the dough and cover loosely with plastic. Cover the bowl with paper towels. Leave in a warm place to allow the dough to rise to double its size, about 1 hour.

3 Make the Raita while the Naan Bread dough is rising, by combining the vegetables, coriander leaves, ground cumin, salt and yogurt in a bowl, stirring to mix well. Serve immediately, or cover and refrigerate up to 1 hour. (If desired, the Raita can be made using cucumber only.)

4 When the Naan Bread dough has risen, divide it into 4 pieces. Shape each into a ball, cover and leave to rise on a lightly floured surface, about 30 minutes. Flatten the balls with your hands, then roll into circles about 7 in (18 cm) in diameter. Place on a floured surface, cover with paper towels and leave to rise until spongy and light to the touch, about 20 minutes. To make Garlic Naan, sprinkle minced garlic and chopped fresh coriander leaves on the dough before cooking. For Kashmiri Naan, sprinkle 2 tablespoons saffron milk (made by soaking ¹/₄ teaspoon saffron threads in 2 tablespoons hot milk), 1 tablespoon sesame seeds and 2 tablespoons raisins on the dough before cooking.

5 Heat a heavy cast iron skillet until hot. Add a piece of dough, cover the pan and cook for 2 minutes. Turn the dough and cook the other side, again with the pan covered. Remove and wrap in a clean dish towel while cooking the remaining Naan Bread. To serve, place the Naan Bread, Banana Chutney, Raita, Green Chili Mango Chutney and the various accompaniments in separate bowls and let guests choose their own dips.

Serves 4–6   Preparation time: 50 mins + rising time for dough   Cooking time: 15 mins

Red rice and tempeh sushi

This is a creative Balinese interpretation of Japanese sushi. For more tropical sushi recipes, see page 44.

2 teaspoons oil
1 small shallot, finely sliced
1 clove garlic, minced
1 bird's-eye chili, deseeded and finely sliced
1 small cake *tempeh* (2 oz/60 g), finely sliced and deep-fried until crisp
2 tablespoons thick sweet soy sauce (*kecap manis*)
2 teaspoons oyster sauce
1 teaspoon shaved palm sugar or dark brown sugar
1/2 teaspoon salt
1 tablespoon tamarind pulp, soaked in 2 tablespoons warm water, mashed and strained to obtain the juice
1/3 cup (50 g) finely sliced cucumber
1/2 cup (100 g) uncooked red or brown rice, boiled until cooked
3/4 cup (75 g) prepared Sushi Rice (page 31)
2 sheets toasted *nori* seaweed measuring 7 x 8 in (18 x 21 cm)

Serves 4
Preparation time: 15 mins
Cooking time: 5 mins

1 Heat the oil in a wok and add the shallot, garlic and chili. Stir-fry over low-medium heat, 3 minutes. Add the deep-fried *tempeh*, thick sweet soy sauce, oyster sauce, palm sugar, salt and tamarind juice and stir-fry until the liquid dries up, about 2 minutes. Remove the mixture with a slotted spoon, leaving any oil in the wok and allow the mixture to cool.

2 Combine the cooked red or brown rice and Sushi Rice, stirring to mix well. Set aside.

3 Place the *nori* sheets on a clean board and arrange half the *tempeh* mixture and cucumber across the center of each sheet. Roll up very firmly and set aside.

4 Wet your hands. Lay a sheet of plastic wrap over a sushi mat and use a spoon to spread half the rice mixture in a rectangle about 5 in (13 cm) wide and 7 in (18 cm) long across the sushi mat, pressing it firmly with the spoon and your hands to make it adhere. Lay one *nori*-wrapped roll in the center. Roll up, squeezing firmly, so that the *nori* roll is completely enclosed by the rice. Set roll aside and repeat with the remaining ingredients to make 1 more roll. Remove the plastic wrap and cut each roll across with a sharp knife into 5 pieces. Serve with pickled ginger, wasabi and soy sauce.

Pita bread pockets

Fresh salad vegetables, accentuated by an accompanying Raita (page 79), are partnered with your choice of beef, chicken, or lamb. When preparing meat recipes for another meal, make sure you cook extra so you'll have plenty extra for these pita sandwiches.

1 portion Raita (page 79).
2 lettuce leaves
2 Chinese (Napa) cabbage leaves
4 pita breads or other Mediterranean breads, cut in half to make 8 pockets
½ ripe tomato, finely sliced
½ small onion, finely sliced
1 teaspoon fresh lime juice
½ teaspoon salt
4 sprigs fresh coriander leaves (cilantro)
4 sprigs mint

FILLING
Grilled Coriander Chicken (page 90), Grilled Rendang Rib-eye Steaks (page 84), or Lemongrass Lamb Chops (page 85), shredded

1 Prepare the main Filling by following any of the recipes listed.

2 Prepare the Raita using the recipe given on page 79.

3 Wash, dry and finely shred the lettuce and Chinese cabbage. Combine the lettuce, cabbage, tomato, onion, lime juice and salt in a bowl, tossing to coat well. Divide this salad between the bread pockets, then add some of the Filling. Garnish with coriander leaves, mint sprigs and sliced red chili and serve with the Raita.

Serves 4
Preparation time: 15 mins
Cooking time: 35 mins

poultry and meat dishes

Grilled rendang rib-eye steaks

Rendang—a Sumatran specialty of beef cooked with chilies, aromatic roots, herbs and spices—is the inspiration for this light, modern recipe. Instead of being simmered in coconut milk, the meat is briefly marinated in a typical Rendang Spice Paste, then grilled to fragrant perfection.

4 thick rib-eye or sirloin steaks, each about 8 oz (250 g)
½ teaspoon salt
¼ teaspoon ground black pepper
1 tablespoon ground coriander
1 tablespoon crushed peppercorns

RENDANG SPICE PASTE
2 tablespoons oil
2 bird's-eye chilies, deseeded
½ in (12 mm) galangal root, sliced
½ in (12 mm) fresh ginger root, sliced
2 small shallots, sliced
1 clove garlic, sliced
1 stalk lemongrass, tender inner part of bottom third only, sliced
2 candlenuts or macadamia nuts, crushed
½ teaspoon ground coriander
¼ teaspoon ground cumin
1 *salam* leaf, torn (optional)
1 kaffir lime leaf, sliced
1–2 red finger-length chilies, deseeded and sliced
¼ cup (60 ml) water

1 To prepare the Rendang Spice Paste, heat the oil in a small pan and add the bird's eye chili, galangal, ginger, shallots, garlic, lemongrass and candlenuts or macadamia nuts. Stir fry over low heat, 4–5 minutes. Add the ground coriander and cumin, *salam* leaf (if using) and kaffir lime leaf. Stir-fry for 1 minute, then remove from the heat. Remove the *salam* leaf but do not discard.

2 Transfer to a blender and process the fried spice paste until smooth. Return the spice paste and *salam* leaf to the pan and add the finely sliced red chilies. Rinse out the blender with the water and add to the pan. Cook the spice paste over low heat, stirring frequently, until the paste is cooked and thick, about 10 minutes; add a little more water from time to time if the paste threatens to stick. Cool and discard the *salam* leaf.

3 Season the beef with the salt, black pepper, coriander and crushed peppercorns. Smear both sides of the meat with the Rendang Spice Paste and set aside to marinate for 30 minutes or longer. Grill over high heat until done to taste. Serve hot.

Serves 4   Preparation time: 20 mins + marinating time   Cooking time: 40 mins

8 lamb loin chops (2 lbs/1 kg), trimmed of excess fat
Ground black pepper, to taste
8 pods fresh or frozen soybeans (edamame) or lima beans, boiled until tender

LEMONGRASS MARINADE
2 teaspoons cumin seeds, lightly roasted
3 in (7.5 cm) fresh ginger root, sliced
1½ in (4 cm) fresh turmeric root, sliced
4 small shallots, sliced
4 cloves garlic, smashed
2 stalks lemongrass, tender inner part of bottom third only, sliced
2 tablespoons sugar
1 teaspoon salt
2 tablespoons oil

Lemongrass lamb chops

The heavenly perfume of lemongrass, processed to a paste with other aromatics and cumin, permeates these lamb chops. As they can be prepared well in advance, they're ideal to serve at a barbecue or picnic and can be accompanied by either baby new potatoes or rice.

1 To prepare the Lemongrass Marinade, grind the cumin seeds to a fine powder in a mortar or blender. Add all the other ingredients except the oil and process to a paste, adding a little of the oil if needed to keep the mixture turning.

2 Heat the oil in a small pan and stir-fry the paste over low heat until fragrant and cooked, 8–10 minutes. Transfer to a bowl and leave to cool.

3 Sprinkle both sides of the lamb chops with a little ground black pepper, then rub generously with the Lemongrass Marinade. Set aside to marinate for 30 minutes or longer. Grill the chops until done to taste and serve garnished with the cooked green soybeans or lima beans.

Serves 4   Preparation time: 15 mins   Cooking time: 30 mins

Black pepper beef

These beef cubes have an excellent flavor and melt-in-the-mouth texture, thanks partly to the technique of flash-frying the beef in boiling oil before stir-frying it. Typical Vietnamese seasonings such as lemongrass and fish sauce join Western sauces to make a sophisticated yet easily prepared dish.

1½ lbs (700 g) tenderloin or fillet steak
Oil, for deep-frying
¼ cup (½ stick/60 g) butter
1 small onion, cut into 8–10 wedges
6–8 cloves garlic, thinly sliced
2 teaspoons coarsely crushed black pepper
2 green onions (scallions)
1 tablespoon Crispy Fried Garlic (page 31)
1 *pappadum*, cut into any shape, to garnish

MARINADE
2 stalks lemongrass, tender inner part of
    bottom third only, finely sliced
½ teaspoon chicken stock bouillon powder
1 teaspoon rice wine (or sherry)
1 teaspoon sugar
1 teaspoon dark soy sauce
1 tablespoon cornstarch or potato starch
2 tablespoons water

SAUCE
3 teaspoons fish sauce
2 teaspoons Worchestershire sauce
1½ teaspoons tomato ketchup
1½ teaspoons sugar
½ teaspoon sesame oil
¼ cup (60 ml) chicken stock

1 Cut the beef into 1-in (2.5-cm) cubes. Put the beef cubes in a bowl. Sprinkle with all the Marinade ingredients, then massage by hand until the liquid is absorbed. Refrigerate in a covered container for at least 2 hours.

2 Slice the white part of the green onions thinly for stir-frying and slice the leaves lengthwise into long strands, to be used as a garnish.

3 Mix all the Sauce ingredients together in a small bowl, stirring until the sugar dissolves, then set aside.

4 Drain the beef cubes and pat them dry with paper towels. Heat the oil in a wok until smoking hot. Deep-fry the marinated beef cubes, a few at a time, for just 10 seconds. Remove with a slotted spoon and drain on paper towels.

5 Remove the oil from the wok and add the butter. Add the onion wedges, garlic and white part of the green onions and stir-fry over high heat for about 30 seconds. Add the black pepper and stir-fry for about 15 seconds, then add the beef and the Sauce and stir-fry over high heat until the beef is just cooked, about 2 minutes. Serve immediately on a bed of green onion leaves and garnish with Crispy Fried Garlic and, if desired, *pappadum*.

Serves 4–5   Preparation time: 10 mins + marinating time   Cooking time: 5 mins

Chicken with sweet soy

This delicious spicy and sweet stir-fry is quick to prepare, making it a great, stress-free weekday dinner. Instead of chicken, this dish can also be prepared with firm tofu.,

¼ cup (60 ml) thick sweet soy sauce (*kecap manis*)
¼ cup (60 ml) soy sauce
2 teaspoons oyster sauce
1 teaspoon sesame oil
2 tablespoons oil
2 small shallots, thinly sliced
2 cloves garlic, minced
1 tablespoon thinly sliced green onion (scallions)
1–2 red finger-length chilies, deseeded and sliced
1 lb (500 g) boneless chicken meat, cubed
Ground white pepper, to taste

1 Combine both soy sauces, oyster sauce and sesame oil in a small bowl and set aside.

2 Heat the oil in a wok and add the shallots, garlic, spring onion and chilies. Stir-fry over high heat, 30 seconds, then add the chicken and stir-fry for another 2 minutes. Add the sauce mixture and continue stir-frying until the chicken is cooked, about 2 minutes. Sprinkle with pepper and serve hot with Coconut Rice with Assorted Side Dishes (page 73).

Serves 4–6   Preparation time: 5 mins   Cooking time: 6 mins

4 small racks of lamb
2 tablespoons butter, melted
Vegetables, for garnishing

MARINADE
1 cup (250 ml) thick plain yogurt
3 tablespoons cream
1 egg yolk
2½ tablespoons minced garlic
2 tablespoon minced fresh ginger root
1 teaspoon salt
2 tablespoons fresh lime or lemon juice
2 teaspoons *garam masala*
2 teaspoons ground red pepper (cayenne)
1 teaspoon ground black pepper
1 teaspoon ground turmeric
2 teaspoons chopped coriander leaves (cilantro)

Barbecued tandoori lamb

Food baked in a tandoor or clay oven in India is usually marinated in a mixture of yogurt (which acts as a tenderizer), plenty of ginger and garlic, plus aromatic spices. This marinade is further enriched with cream and egg yolk and the barbecued items served on a bed of freshly cut vegetables. If you prefer, the meat can be marinated for as long as 24 hours in advance.

1 To prepare the Marinade, put the yogurt in a bowl and stir in the cream and egg yolk. Grind the garlic, ginger, salt and lime juice to a paste in a mortar or spice grinder, then add to the yogurt mixture. Stir in the other ingredients and set aside.

2 Remove the skin from the racks of lamb and prick the meat all over to allow the Marinade to penetrate. Rub the meat with the Marinade, cover and refrigerate at least 3 hours, or overnight.

3 Cook the lamb over a charcoal grill, turning until golden brown on all sides and cooked, or roast in a 350°F (180°C) oven for about 20 minutes for medium-rare lamb. When the meat is cooked, brush all over with the butter. Return to the charcoal grill or oven for another 2 minutes.

4 Serve on a bed of freshly cut vegetables like carrots, cucumber, lettuce and jicama or daikon.

Serves 4   Preparation time: 15 mins + marinating time   Cooking time: 30 mins

Tropical beef steaks

Semur, a Dutch-inspired dish of braised beef simmered in an exciting sauce accented with soy sauce, coriander and freshly grated nutmeg, is given a modern twist in this recipe. Sirloin steaks are used instead of stewing beef, with some of the usual seasonings used in the marinade, while others appear in the accompanying sauce. This truly delicious sauce—which is so good you'll never eat steak any other way—can be prepared in advance to save time.

¹/₄ cup (60 ml) soy sauce
¹/₃ cup (80 ml) water
1 tablespoon sugar
2 teaspoons coriander seeds, roasted and coarsely crushed (see note)
3–4 cloves garlic, minced
4 sirloin or fillet steaks, each about 6–8 oz (180–250 g), fat trimmed
2 teaspoons oil
Sprigs of watercress, to garnish

FRAGRANT SAUCE
1½ tablespoons oil
5–6 small shallots, sliced
4–5 cloves garlic, minced
1–2 red finger-length chilies, deseeded and sliced
1 bird's-eye chili, deseeded and sliced
2 teaspoons minced galangal root
2 teaspoons minced fresh ginger root
1 cup (250 ml) chicken stock
1 teaspoon ground coriander
4 whole cloves
¹/₄ teaspoon freshly grated nutmeg
¹/₃ cup (80 ml) thick sweet soy sauce (*kecap manis*)
4 teaspoons soy sauce
Salt and pepper, to taste

NOTE: Do not use ground coriander for the beef marinade if you can avoid it as the taste is very different. Use whole coriander seeds that are lightly roasted in a dry pan and then coarsely crushed for a superior flavor and texture.

1 Combine the soy sauce, water, sugar, crushed coriander seeds and garlic in a bowl, stirring to mix well. Add the steaks and set aside to marinate for about 25 minutes, turning the steaks a couple of times.

2 To prepare the Fragrant Sauce, heat the oil in a small pan and add the shallots, garlic, chilies, galangal and ginger. Stir-fry over low heat for 10 minutes. Add ¹/₂ cup (125 ml) of the stock and the ground coriander and cloves. Bring to a boil and simmer for 2–3 minutes. Cool, then process in a blender until smooth. Return to the saucepan, add the remaining chicken stock, nutmeg and thick sweet soy sauce. Cover and simmer for 15 minutes. Add the soy sauce, taste and add salt and pepper if desired.

3 Heat the oil in a non-stick or cast-iron pan until very hot. Add the steaks and sear on both sides. Lower the heat slightly and cook to taste. Pour over the Fragrant Sauce, stir for a few seconds to heat through, then transfer the beef to a serving dish. Garnish with sprigs of land or watercress.

Serves 4   Preparation time: 10 mins + marinating time   Cooking time: 40 mins

Grilled coriander chicken

A delicious marinade with a balance of herbs and spices is the secret
to preparing flavorful and moist grilled meats, and in particular grilled
chicken breasts, which tend to dry out. This simple recipe—inspired
by Indian cuisine—will give you moist and flavorful chicken every time.
Served in a hot pita pocket, this makes a satisfying lunch.

4 free range chicken breasts
6–8 baby leeks, grilled

MARINADE
4 teaspoons coriander seeds, lightly roasted
4 teaspoons cumin seeds, lightly roasted
5–6 cloves garlic, minced
**2 tablespoons finely chopped fresh coriander
    leaves (cilantro)**
2–3 teaspoons paprika
1–2 teaspoons ground red pepper (cayenne)
1 teaspoon salt
¼ teaspoon ground black pepper
2 tablespoons oil

1 To make the Marinade, first dry-roast the
coriander and cumin seeds in a skillet over
low-medium heat until they become fragrant,
then process the seeds to a fine powder in a
spice grinder. Transfer to a bowl and stir in all
the other ingredients. Spread both sides of
the chicken breasts with the Marinade and set
aside for 30 minutes or longer.

2 Brush a grill pan with oil and cook the
chicken breasts over medium heat, turning
to cook both sides. Serve on a bed of grilled
baby leeks, or as a filling for Pita Bread Pockets
(page 81).

Serves 4
Preparation time: 15 mins + marinating time
Cooking time: 30 mins

Tender poached ginger chicken

This recipe features a medley of meaty shiitake mushrooms, delicate Japanese nameko and shimeji mushrooms, and long slender enoki mushrooms. These are all stir-fried and served with chicken breasts that have been poached in a ginger-flavored stock for a light and healthy gourmet meal.

4 free range chicken breasts
2–3 cups (500–750 ml) chicken stock
4 in (10 cm) fresh ginger root, bruised
4 sprigs coriander leaves (cilantro) and roots
Salt and ground white pepper, to taste
1 bunch (4 oz/125 g) watercress sprigs
1 tomato, peeled and finely diced
2 tablespoons finely sliced chives

MUSHROOM MEDLEY
2 tablespoons olive oil
1 tablespoon vegetable oil
2 cloves garlic, minced
5–6 fresh shiitake mushrooms, sliced
3½ oz (100 g) shimeji mushrooms
2 oz (50 g) nameko mushrooms
2 oz (50 g) enoki mushrooms
¼ teaspoon salt
Ground black pepper, to taste
2 tablespoons mushroom oyster sauce or
    regular oyster sauce

NOTE: If not all these mushrooms are available, use a mixture of fresh mushrooms such as straw mushrooms, oyster mushrooms, Swiss brown mushrooms, or portobello mushrooms; the use of canned mushrooms is not recommended. If you like, the remaining ginger-flavored chicken stock could be used as a soup to accompany the chicken; add some sliced green onions or cubes of soft tofu.

1 Place the chicken breasts, stock, ginger and coriander in a saucepan and bring almost to a boil. Taste and add salt and pepper as desired. Cover the pan and poach over low heat, with the water just below simmering stage, until the chicken is cooked, about 20 minutes. Remove from the heat but leave the chicken in the stock.

2 Prepare the Mushroom Medley. Heat both lots of oil in a wok and add the garlic. Stir-fry over high heat 10 seconds, then add the shiitake mushrooms and stir-fry for 1 minute. Add the remaining mushrooms and stir-fry until cooked, about 2 minutes. Season with salt, pepper and oyster sauce, stir well, then divide between 4 serving plates.

3 Add a warm chicken breast to each plate, spoon over some of the stock and garnish with watercress and tomatoes. Sprinkle with chives and serve immediately.

Serves 4   Preparation time: 10 mins   Cooking time: 35 mins

1½ lbs (700 g) top round beef
30 bamboo skewers, soaked in water for 2
   hours before using
1 portion Peanut Satay Sauce (page 26)

SPICE PASTE
4 candlenuts or macadamia nuts, roughly
   chopped
2 in (5 cm) galangal root, peeled and sliced
1 in (2.5 cm) fresh ginger root, peeled and sliced
2–3 red finger-length chilies, deseeded
5 small shallots, peeled
3 cloves garlic, peeled
½ teaspoon ground black pepper
1 teaspoon coriander seeds or ½ teaspoon
   ground coriander
3 tablespoons shaved palm sugar or dark
   brown sugar
1 teaspoon salt
2 tablespoons oil
1 *salam* leaf

Fragrant beef satay

Satay consists of bite-sized chunks of meat on bamboo skewers grilled over a grill pan or broiler and served with peanut sauce. Here, the meat is seasoned and marinated overnight before grilling.

1 Cut the beef into 1-in (2.5-cm) cubes and set aside.

2 Make the Spice Paste by grinding all the ingredients, except the oil and *salam* leaf, to a paste in a mortar or blender, adding a little oil if necessary to keep the mixture turning. Heat the oil in a wok over medium heat and stir-fry the ground paste with the *salam* leaf for 3 to 5 minutes until fragrant. Remove from the heat and set aside to cool.

3 When cooled, place the Spice Paste and beef in a large bowl and mix well. Set aside in the refrigerator to marinate overnight.

4 Soak the bamboo skewers in water for 2 hours before using so they do not burn when grilling the meat. Thread the marinated beef onto the skewers and grill over hot charcoal or under a preheated oven broiler for 2 to 3 minutes on each side, basting with the marinade, until cooked. Turn the skewers frequently to prevent the beef from burning, it should be browned on the outside and cooked on the inside. Arrange the satay on a serving platter and serve with a bowl of Peanut Satay Sauce on the side.

Serves 4   Preparation time: 10 mins   Cooking time: 25 mins

Barbecued baby back spareribs

These succulent pork ribs are simmered in court bouillon with Chinese spices, then drenched in a richly flavored barbecue sauce before being grilled. If you can't obtain racks of baby back pork ribs, use meaty pork shoulder ribs. If you do not have time to make the barbecue sauce, use a commercial brand of sauce.

8½ cups (2 liters) court bouillon (see note)
2 pods star anise
½ teaspoon five spice powder
4 sides baby back pork ribs, each about 1½ lbs (700 g), or 4–5 lbs (2–2½ kg) meaty pork shoulder ribs
1 portion Fennel and Pumpkin Slaw (page 67), for serving

BARBECUE SAUCE
2 tablespoons oil
2 small onions, sliced
2 tablespoons minced garlic
1 can (13 oz/400 g) chopped tomatoes with juice
1¼ cups (310 ml) white vinegar
4 tablespoons brown sugar
1 tablespoon salt
1 tablespoon ground black pepper
1 tablespoon paprika
1 tablespoon ground red pepper (cayenne)
1 tablespoon molasses
1 tablespoon hoisin sauce
½ cup (125 ml) orange juice
2 tablespoons English mustard powder

NOTE: If fresh or powdered court bouillon is not available, use light chicken stock with 1 teaspoon vinegar added.

1 To make the Barbecue Sauce, heat the oil in a large pan and add the onion. Stir-fry over medium heat until golden brown, then add all the other ingredients. Bring to a boil, stirring several times, then reduce the heat and simmer uncovered over very low heat, about 2 hours. Cool, then process to a purée.

2 While the Sauce is simmering, bring the court bouillon, star anise and five spice powder to a boil in a large saucepan. Cover and simmer for 10 minutes, then add the pork ribs and simmer until tender, 1–1½ hours. Drain and allow to cool.

3 Put the pork ribs in a large bowl and pour the Barbecue Sauce over them. Toss to coat the ribs thoroughly, then grill lightly over hot charcoal or under a preheated oven broiler until fragrant and browned.

Serves 4   Preparation time: 15 mins   Cooking time: 4 hours

seafood dishes

Pan-fried fish fillets with diced mango

The sweetness, smooth texture and fragrance of fresh mango is perhaps the most striking feature of this easily prepared recipe. Pan-fried fish is served on a bed of rice vermicelli, and herb and mango salad, which has a Thai accent in the fish sauce, chili and lime dressing. The refreshing flavors of this recipe make it ideal for a warm summer evening.

1 large ripe firm mango
$^1/_3$ cup (80 ml) fish sauce
$2^1/_2$ tablespoons fresh lime juice
4 teaspoons superfine sugar
$^1/_4$ teaspoon sesame oil
4 fresh white fish fillets, such as black cod, garoupa or sea bass, about 5 oz (150 g) each, deboned and skinned
1 teaspoon salt
Liberal sprinkling of ground white pepper
2 tablespoons cornstarch
3 tablespoons oil
Fresh sprigs of coriander leaves (cilantro) and dill, to garnish

SALAD
5 oz (150 g) dried rice vermicelli (*beehoon* or *mifen*), soaked in warm water until soft, then drained
1 small red onion, halved lengthwise and finely sliced across
2 small shallots, thinly sliced
$1^1/_2$ tablespoons finely sliced fresh young ginger root
1–2 bird's-eye chilies, deseeded and sliced
3 tablespoons finely sliced green onions (scallions)
3 tablespoons finely chopped fresh coriander leaves (cilantro) and stems, or mint leaves

1 To prepare the Salad, bring a saucepan of water to a boil, add the drained vermicelli and cook just 1 minute. Drain and cool, then transfer to a bowl and add the onion, shallot, ginger, chilies, green onions and coriander leaves and stems (or mint leaves). Toss gently to mix.

2 Cut the mango in half lengthwise (around the stone), then use a spoon to scoop out the flesh from each half. Cut half the flesh into fine strips and the remainder into $^1/_2$-in (12-mm) dice.

3 Combine the fish sauce, lime juice, sugar and sesame oil in a small bowl and stir until the sugar dissolves. Pour the mixture over the Salad, add the mango strips and toss gently. Divide the Salad into 4 serving plates and set aside while preparing the fish.

4 Put the fish on a plate and sprinkle both sides with salt, pepper and cornstarch. Shake the fish to remove the excess cornstarch. Heat the oil in a skillet and fry the fish over high heat, turning, until golden brown on both sides and cooked through, about 6 minutes. Drain the fish on paper towels, then place on top of each portion of Salad. Garnish with the diced mango, coriander leaves and stems, and dill, before serving.

Serves 4   Preparation time: 20 mins   Cooking time: 20 mins

Barbecued jumbo shrimp with vindaloo dip

Vindaloo, a fiery curry dish from Goa, on the west coast of India, is characterized by plenty of garlic, chilies, vinegar and spices. In this modern version, a Vindaloo Dip is prepared and served as a dipping sauce with marinated grilled jumbo shrimp to make a delicious tropical meal.

12–16 fresh jumbo shrimp, peeled and deveined, final tail sections left intact
2 cups mixed salad greens and herbs, such as arugula, torn Romaine or cos lettuce, green onions (scallions) and sprigs of fresh mint and coriander leaves (cilantro)
1 portion Vindaloo Dip (page 28), for dipping

MARINADE
4 cloves garlic, minced
$^{3}/_{4}$ in (2 cm) fresh ginger root, sliced
1 teaspoon salt
1–2 teaspoons ground red pepper (cayenne)
1 teaspoon ground turmeric
$1^{1}/_{2}$ tablespoons fresh lime juice

1 Prepare the Vindaloo Dip using the recipe on page 28.

2 Prepare the Marinade by pounding or processing the garlic, ginger and salt to a paste. Transfer to a bowl and stir in the ground red pepper, turmeric and lime juice. Add the shrimp and toss to coat well. Marinate in the refrigerator for 30 minutes.

3 Heat a grill or broiler. Cook the shrimp over high heat, turning to cook both sides, about 3–4 minutes on each side, depending on the size of the shrimp. Place the salad greens on a serving plate and arrange the shrimp on top. Reheat the Vindaloo Dip and serve as a dipping sauce.

Serves 4–6
Preparation time: 10 mins + marinating time
Cooking time: 15 mins

4 fresh tuna steaks (each about 7 oz/200 g
    and 1-in/2.5-cm) thick
1 teaspoon salt
1 tablespoon fresh lime juice
4 cloves garlic, minced
1½ tablespoons curry powder
1–2 tablespoons oil
Fresh coriander leaf sprigs (cilantro)

TROPICAL FRUIT SALSA
1 mandarin orange
1 ripe mango
¼ ripe sweet pineapple
Flesh of ¼ coconut, sliced
Sugar, to taste

Serves 4
Preparation time: 15 mins + marinating time
Cooking time: 20 mins

Seared tuna steaks with tropical fruit salsa

This recipe is incredibly easy but so good nobody will believe that it takes less than 5 minutes to prepare the fish, plus 1 hour marinating. The sweet and sour tang of the Citrus Salsa adds a delightful piquancy and freshness that complements the rich spicy tuna perfectly.

1 Place the fish on a plate and sprinkle both sides with salt and lime juice. Scatter one side with some of the garlic, then with some of the curry powder, pressing to make it adhere to the fish. Turn and season the second side with garlic and curry powder. Cover and allow to marinate 1 hour in the refrigerator.

2 While the tuna is marinating, prepare the Tropical Fruit Salsa. Peel all the fruit and remove the coverings of the orange segments. Diced the peeled fruit. Combine in a bowl, stirring to mix well. Taste and add sugar if necessary. Cover and refrigerate until ready to serve.

3 Heat a charcoal grill or oven broiler (a stovetop grill pan can also be used). Brush both sides of the fish with oil and cook, about 4 minutes on each side. Serve with the Tropical Fruit Salsa. Garnish with coriander leaves.

Singapore chili crab

One of the all-time great seafood dishes of tropical Asia, Singapore Chili Crab is an irresistible feast of succulent fresh crab still in the shell, dripping with a hot spicy sauce which is thickened with beaten egg and cornstarch. It is best enjoyed with chunks of French bread or steamed rice to soak up the rich sauce. Don't forget to serve with nut-crackers and finger bowls as this is a hands-on dish!

4 lbs (2 kg) fresh uncooked crabs
Oil, for deep-frying
6–7 small shallots, finely sliced
8–10 cloves garlic, minced
3 tablespoons minced fresh ginger root
3–4 bird's-eye chilies, sliced
3½ cups (875 ml) chicken stock
3–4 tablespoons fermented bean paste (see note)
¼ cup (60 ml) bottled sweet chili sauce
½ cup (125 ml) tomato ketchup
1 tablespoon sugar
2½ tablespoons rice wine or sherry
2 teaspoons salt
1 teaspoon ground white pepper
2 tablespoons cornstarch, mixed with 3 tablespoons water
2 eggs, lightly beaten
1 green onion (scallion), cut into short lengths
French bread or other soft bread, for serving

CHILI GINGER SAUCE
½ teaspoon salt
4–6 red finger-length chilies, deseeded and sliced
5–6 cloves garlic
2 tablespoons minced fresh ginger root
2 teaspoons sugar
1 teaspoon rice vinegar or ½ teaspoon white vinegar
1 teaspoon water

1 If the crabs are alive, stun them by putting them in the freezer for 15–20 minutes. Cut in half lengthwise with a cleaver and remove the backs and spongy matter from the shells. Remove the claws from the body and crack with a cleaver in several places. Cut each body half into 2–3 pieces, leaving legs attached. Wash (scrub with a soft brush if necessary), drain thoroughly and pat completely dry.

2 Prepare the Chili Ginger Sauce by blending all the ingredients to a paste in a mortar or blender. Set aside.

3 Heat the oil in a wok until very hot. Have the wok cover or a large lid handy to hold over the wok. Add the crab pieces, a few at a time and deep-fry for 2 minutes, holding the lid above the oil as it will splutter. Drain the crab pieces well and set aside. Remove all but 2 tablespoons of oil from the wok.

4 Reheat the oil and add the shallots, garlic, ginger and chilies. Stir-fry over low-medium heat until fragrant, about 3 minutes, then add the chicken stock, bean paste, Chili Ginger Sauce, bottled sweet chili sauce, tomato ketchup, sugar, rice wine or sherry, salt and pepper. Bring to a boil, lower the heat and simmer for 2 minutes. Add the crab pieces and simmer until cooked, 3–4 minutes.

5 Stir in the cornstarch mixture, and continue stirring until the sauce thickens and clears. Add the eggs and stir until set, then transfer the dish to a serving platter. Garnish with green onion and serve with French bread or steamed rice.

NOTE: Fermented bean paste is made with fermented soybeans, *tau cheo*, and is sometimes labelled "salted soya beans" or "yellow bean sauce," often with additional chili and seasonings added. Any sort of bean paste may be used although you may need to adjust the other seasonings if it is very spicy or sweet.

Serves 4–5   Preparation time: 20 mins   Cooking time: 20 mins

4 in (10 cm) fresh ginger, sliced
5 cloves garlic
1 teaspoon salt
2 teaspoons ground turmeric
2 teaspoons fresh lime juice
1½ lbs (700 g) white fish fillets, cut into cubes
3 tablespoons oil
10 cardamom pods, slit and bruised
1 teaspoon brown mustard seeds
1 teaspoon cumin seeds
1 small onion, thinly sliced
1 pandanus leaf, raked with a fork and tied in
  a knot
12 curry leaves
2–3 teaspoons ground red pepper (cayenne)
1 teaspoon ground coriander
1½ tablespoons water
1 ripe tomato, sliced
1¾ cups (400 ml) coconut milk
¾ cup (150 g) fresh or canned pineapple cubes
Salt, to taste
1 green finger-length chili, deseeded and sliced

Heavenly fish and pineapple curry

This curry has a lovely combination of flavors, with cubes of fish
simmered in a richly spiced curry gravy softened with coconut milk and
fresh pineapple for added fragrance and a sweet-sour tang. Any fish with
firm-textured white flesh is suitable for this dish.

1 Pound or process the ginger, garlic and salt to make a paste. Mix half of this paste with the
ground turmeric and lime juice, then transfer to a bowl and add the fish, tossing gently to coat
all over. Set aside. Reserve the remaining paste for use in step 2.

2 Heat the oil in a saucepan and add the cardamoms, mustard and cumin seeds, and stir-fry
over high heat until they pop. Remove half of the spices and oil and set aside to be added to
the cooked dish later. Add the onion, pandanus leaf and curry leaves to the saucepan and stir-
fry until the onion is light brown, 3–4 minutes. Add the reserved ginger-garlic paste and stir-fry
for 2 more minutes.

3 Combine the ground red pepper and ground coriander with the water in a small bowl,
mixing to make a paste. Add to the pan and stir-fry until fragrant, 2 minutes.

4 Add the tomato and cook, uncovered, stirring several times, until very soft, about 5 minutes.
Add the coconut milk gradually, scraping the bottom of the pan to dislodge any spices. Bring
to a boil, stirring, then add the marinated fish and pineapple cubes, and simmer until the fish
is cooked, 6–7 minutes. Taste and add salt if needed. Discard the pandanus leaf, add the sliced
green chili and reserved fried spices, and serve hot with steamed white rice.

Serves 4–5   Preparation time: 20 mins   Cooking time: 30 mins

Steamed snapper with lemongrass

Steamed fish is one of the highlights of Chinese cuisine and for the best results, the fish must be absolutely fresh. In this recipe—which combines fragrant tropical Asian seasonings with spicy Sichuan pickled vegetable—fresh whole fish are steamed in a delicate crab stock perfumed with lemongrass (see Note).

1 whole red snapper, about 2 lbs (1 kg), cleaned and scaled, or four 7-oz (200-g) snapper fillets
1 green onion (scallion), cut into lengths
4 slices lime or lemon
3/4 cup (100 g) pickled Sichuan vegetable (*za cai*), tough outer skin removed, rinsed and thinly sliced
4 red or green finger-length chilies, deseeded and split lengthwise, to garnish
1 lime, quartered, to serve

LEMONGRASS BROTH
4 lbs (2 kg) fresh uncooked crabs
3–5 red bird's-eye chilies
6 cloves garlic, peeled and left whole
4 small shallots, peeled and left whole
5 stalks lemongrass, tender inner part of bottom third only, bruised
1/2 cup (20 g) chopped fresh coriander leaves (cilantro) and stems
8 1/2 cups (2 liters) water
Salt and ground white pepper, to taste

NOTE: The crab-infused Lemongrass Broth is truly delicious and well worth the time and effort required to prepare it but for a quick and easy alternative, replace the crabs and water with 2 cups (500 ml) chicken or fish stock and 2 cups (500 ml) water

1 Prepare the Lemongrass Broth first. Cut the crabs in half with a cleaver and remove the backs and spongy matter. Remove the claws from the body and crack with a cleaver in several places. Cut each body half into 2–3 pieces, leaving the legs attached. Wash, drain thoroughly and pat completely dry. Put the crab pieces, chilies, garlic, shallots and lemongrass on a baking tray and cook at 425°F (220°C) for 3 minutes. Transfer to a pot, add the coriander leaves, stems and water. Bring to a boil. Boil uncovered, pressing on the crab pieces from time to time, for 30 minutes, or until the liquid is reduced by half. Strain, pressing down firmly on the crab to obtain as much stock as possible. Add the salt and pepper to taste.

2 Place the green onion, lime or lemon slices, and Sichuan pickled vegetable in the bottom of a heatproof dish large enough to hold the fish, and put the fish on top. Pour in enough stock to barely cover the fish and place the bowl on top of a steamer rack set in a wok or steamer pot, above boiling water. Cover and steam over rapidly boiling water until the fish is cooked (the flesh should be white when tested with the tip of a knife), 10–15 minutes (about 20 minutes for one large fish). Transfer to a serving plate, garnish with lime wedges and chili and serve immediately with steamed white rice.

Serves 4   Preparation time: 15 mins   Cooking time: 1 hour

Tropical seafood curry with coconut milk

Seafood seems to have a special affinity for coconut milk, and the spicy coconut gravy bathing this dish of shrimp and calamari is surprisingly light, thanks to the addition of fish or chicken stock. Plenty of chilies, turmeric, galangal and ginger are added to the sauce, but as the chili seeds are discarded, you get all the flavor with minimal heat. Serve this with steamed white rice and a tangy side salad and you have a delicious and satisfying meal.

7 oz (200 g) calamari or baby squid

10 oz (300 g) fresh medium shrimp, peeled and deveined, tail section left intact

1 small zucchini, skin left on, cut into ¼-in (6-mm) strips, blanched 1 minute

1 cup (150 g) sliced green beans, blanched 1 minute

1 red finger-length chili, deseeded and sliced

1 green finger-length chili, deseeded and sliced

¾ cup (180 ml) thick coconut milk

Salt, to taste

Liberal sprinkling of ground black pepper

TURMERIC COCONUT GRAVY

5–6 red finger-length chilies, deseeded and sliced

5–6 small shallots, sliced

1½ in (4 cm) turmeric root, peeled and sliced

¾ in (2 cm) galangal root, peeled and sliced

½ in (12 mm) fresh ginger root, peeled and sliced

2 tablespoons oil

1 tablespoon tamarind pulp, soaked in ¼ cup (60 ml) warm water, mashed and strained to obtain the juice

1 cup (250 ml) fish stock or light chicken stock

1 Prepare the Turmeric Coconut Gravy by processing the chilies, shallots, turmeric, galangal and ginger to a paste in a mortar or blender, adding a little water if necessary to keep the blades turning. Heat the oil in a saucepan and add the paste and stir-fry over low-medium heat until fragrant, 4–5 minutes. Add the tamarind juice and fish stock, bring to a boil, then simmer until slightly thickened, about 10 minutes.

2 Cut the bodies of the squid in half lengthwise and make a crosshatch pattern by scoring the soft inside of the squid pieces with diagonal lines using a very sharp knife, taking care not to cut right through the flesh. Turn the piece of squid and score diagonally across the lines already made, resulting in a crisscross pattern. Cut each squid half into bite-sized pieces.

3 Reheat the Turmeric Coconut Gravy, then add the calamari, shrimp, vegetables and chilies. Bring to a boil, then simmer uncovered for 2 minutes. Add the coconut milk and cook, stirring several times, for another 3 minutes. Taste and add salt and pepper, if desired. Serve hot with steamed rice.

Serves 4–6   Preparation time: 20 mins   Cooking time: 25 mins

4 baby snapper, grouper or bream fillets, each around 7 oz (200 g)
1 teaspoon salt
Dash of ground white pepper
1 tablespoon finely chopped fresh coriander leaves (cilantro)
¼ cup (60 ml) oil
8 cherry tomatoes, or 1 large tomato cut into 8 wedges
2–3 bird's-eye chilies, left whole
8 sprigs lemon basil

FRAGRANT SAUCE
2 tablespoons oil
6–8 red finger-length chilies, some or all of the seeds discarded, sliced
2–3 bird's-eye chilies, deseeded and sliced
8 cloves garlic
1¼ in (3 cm) fresh ginger root, thinly sliced
2 stalks lemongrass, tender inner part of bottom third only, cut into 3 pieces
2 kaffir lime leaves, edges torn
1½ cups (375 ml) water
½ teaspoon salt

Fish fillets in fragrant curry

Inspired by the legendary *Ikan Dabu-dabu* of the eastern Indonesian Spice Islands, this recipe is particularly fragrant, thanks to the use of ginger, garlic, lemongrass, lemon basil and kaffir lime leaves.

1 To prepare the Fragrant Sauce, heat the oil in a small saucepan and add the chilies, garlic and ginger. Stir-fry over low heat until fragrant, 3–4 minutes. Add the lemongrass, kafir lime leaves, water and salt, and simmer 10 minutes. Discard the lemongrass and kaffir lime leaves and process to a smooth sauce. Set aside.

2 Season both sides of the fish with the salt, pepper and coriander leaves. Heat the oil in a skillet, then sear the fish for 2 minutes on each side. Add the tomatoes and cook for a few seconds, shaking the pan. Pour in the Fragrant Sauce and add the chilies. Simmer gently for 3 minutes, then add the lemon basil sprigs. Continue simmering until the fish is cooked through, another 2–3 minutes, depending on the thickness of the fish. Serve hot with steamed rice.

Serves 4   Preparation time: 10 mins   Cooking time: 30 mins

Grilled whole snapper

This marinated barbecued fish recipe is from the Tabanan area of Bali, Indonesia, once the seat of a great raja. The marinade—a superb blend of shallots, garlic, chilies and aromatics—gives the fish a heady fragrance and flavor which is further enhanced by the accompanying Lemongrass Sambal.

1 whole fresh snapper, (about 3 lbs/1½ kg), cleaned and scaled
½ teaspoon salt
Liberal sprinkling of ground white pepper
1 portion Lemongrass Sambal (page 24)
2 limes, halved, to garnish

MARINADE
¼ cup (60 ml) oil
8–10 small shallots, sliced
4–5 cloves garlic, sliced
8–10 red finger-length chilies, deseeded and sliced
2 bird's-eye chilies, deseeded and sliced
1½ tablespoons minced galangal root
2 ripe tomatoes, chopped
2 teaspoons dried shrimp paste (*belachan*), dry-roasted
3 stalks lemongrass, tender inner part of bottom third only, finely sliced
2 *salam* leaves (optional)
1 teaspoon salt
¼ teaspoon ground black pepper
2 teaspoons fresh lime juice

Serves 4
Preparation time: 20 mins + marinating time
Cooking time: 50 mins

1 Prepare the Marinade by heating the oil in a small pan and adding the shallots and garlic. Stir-fry over low heat, 3 minutes, then add the chilies, galangal, tomatoes, dried shrimp paste, lemongrass and *salam* leaves (if using). Cook uncovered, stirring occasionally, about 10 minutes. Remove from the heat, cool, then process until smooth. Transfer to a bowl and stir in the salt, pepper and lime juice.

2 Make 3–4 deep diagonal cuts on both sides of the fish, then sprinkle both sides with salt and pepper. Spread a little of the Marinade inside the fish cavity, then on both sides, pushing it well into the cuts. Set aside to marinate for 20–30 minutes.

3 Grill the fish over hot charcoal or under a preheated oven broiler for 10 minutes. Turn and continue cooking until the fish is thoroughly cooked, another 10–20 minutes. Test with the point of a knife to ensure the fish is white in the center before serving. Serve with Lemongrass Sambal and lime wedges.

Sesame and shrimp crusted tuna chunks

The rich, almost meaty flavor of fresh tuna is best appreciated either raw or lightly cooked. In this recipe, the tuna is first coated in Japanese soybean or miso paste, covered with a lightly seasoned shrimp meat paste then coated with sesame seeds. Deep-fried until the outside is crunchy and golden and the inside still meltingly tender, the tuna cubes can be served with a side-salad of beans tossed in a Sesame Soy Dressing, or speared with toothpicks and enjoyed with a Wasabi Mayonnaise Dip (see page 27).

1 tablespoon miso paste
10 oz (300 g) fresh tuna, cut into 1-in (2.5-cm) cubes
7 oz (200 g) fresh shrimp, peeled and deveined
2 egg whites
1 tablespoon cornstarch
2 teaspoons fresh lime juice
1 teaspoon soy sauce
1 clove garlic, minced
¹/₂ teaspoon salt
Liberal sprinkling of ground white pepper
³/₄ cup (120 g) black and white sesame seeds
1¹/₂ cups (150 g) sliced green beans, blanched and drained
1 portion Sesame Soy Dressing (page 27)
Oil, for deep-frying
1 portion Wasabi Mayonnaise Dip (page 27)

NOTE: Miso paste keeps for many months if refrigerated. It may dry out after storing for some time; if this happens, mix it with 1–2 teaspoons warm water before tossing with the tuna.

1 Put the miso paste in a bowl. Add the tuna and mix by hand to coat well. Set aside.

2 Process the shrimp in a food processor until coarsely ground. Add the egg whites, cornstarch, lime juice, soy sauce, garlic, salt and pepper and blend to make a paste. Add to the tuna and toss to coat. Form the shrimp and spices around the tuna with your hand.

3 Put the sesame seeds in a separate bowl. Coat each piece of tuna on all sides with the sesame seeds, so that they form a crust. Refrigerate 30 minutes.

4 Toss the sliced green beans in the Sesame Soy Dressing and set aside.

5 Heat the oil in a wok and deep-fry the tuna pieces over very high heat just until the sesame seeds turn golden brown, about 1–1¹/₂ minutes. Drain on paper towels and serve with the tossed green beans and Wasabi Mayonnaise Dip.

Serves 4–6   Preparation time: 20 mins + refrigerating time   Cooking time: 5 mins

4 snapper fillets, each about 7 oz (200 g)
Salt and pepper, to taste
4 teaspoons lime or lemon juice
4 pieces banana leaf, each about 9 in (23 cm) square, softened in boiling water, or 4 pieces aluminum foil
1 green tomato, sliced
2 kaffir lime leaves, halved
2 tablespoons lemon basil leaves
1 *salam* leaf, cut in 4 (optional)
1 portion Lemongrass Sambal (page 24)

SPICE PASTE
2 tablespoons oil
8–10 small shallots, finely sliced
4–5 cloves garlic, minced
2 red or green bird's-eye chilies, sliced
1 tablespoon minced galangal root
1 tablespoon minced fresh ginger root
1/2 teaspoon ground turmeric
3 stalks lemongrass, tender inner part of bottom third only, finely sliced
1 teaspoon dried shrimp paste (*belachan*), dry-roasted
2 teaspoons shaved palm sugar or dark brown sugar
1 tablespoon tamarind pulp, soaked in 1/4 cup (60 ml) warm water, mashed and strained to obtain the juice
1/2 teaspoon salt
Ground black pepper, to taste

Serves 4
Preparation time: 20 mins
Cooking time: 40 mins

Spicy grilled fish fillets

Pepes ikan—fish slathered with a fragrant spice paste and wrapped in banana leaf for steaming or grilling—is one of the most delicious dishes in the Balinese culinary repertoire. The spice paste can be prepared in advance and refrigerated, but for maximum fragrance, the accompanying Lemongrass Sambal should be made only while the fish is grilling.

1 Prepare the Spice Paste first. Heat the oil in a small pan and add the shallots, garlic, chilies, galangal, ginger, turmeric, lemongrass and dried shrimp paste. Stir-fry over low-medium heat until fragrant, 4–5 minutes. Add the remaining ingredients and cook, stirring frequently until soft, 6–8 minutes. Cool, then grind or process to a paste.

2 Place the fish fillets on a plate and season on both sides with salt, pepper and lime juice. Spread the Spice Paste evenly over both sides of each fillet. Place a piece of banana leaf on a clean work surface and put a fish fillet diagonally across the leaf. Top with some of the tomato, half a kaffir lime leaf, some of the lemon basil leaves and a quarter of the *salam* leaf. Fold over the end closest to you, tuck in the sides and then turn over to enclose the filling. Repeat with the remaining fish fillets.

3 Place the banana leaf packages over hot charcoal or under an oven broiler and grill on both sides until the fish is done, about 8 minutes, depending on the thickness of the fish. Serve the fish in its banana leaf package (diners must unwrap the leaf, it cannot be eaten), accompanied by Lemongrass Sambal and steamed white rice.

Crunchy batter-fried shrimp

Shrimp dipped in a flavorful crunchy batter containing chopped peanuts are deep-fried in this unusual recipe. The accompanying Green Mango Salad has a sweet-sour tang and contrasts beautifully with the shrimp.

1 Peel the shrimp, leaving the tail section intact. Discard the heads and shells and cut open the back of each shrimp to remove the intestinal tract. Set the shrimp aside.

2 Process the candlenuts, garlic, turmeric and ginger until finely ground, adding a little water, if necessary, to keep the mixture turning. Put the spice paste in a bowl and whisk in 1/2 cup (125 ml) water and the beaten egg. Set aside.

3 Combine the rice flour, cornstarch, pepper, ground coriander, salt and kaffir lime leaves in a separate bowl, stirring well to mix. Slowly stir in the water and spice paste mixture, adding a little more water if needed to make a thick batter. Stir in the chopped peanuts.

4 Heat the oil in a wok until very hot. Hold a shrimp by the tail and dip it in the peanut batter to coat all over. Carefully slip it into the hot oil and fry the shrimp, a few at a time, until crisp and golden brown, about 3 minutes. Drain on paper towels and keep warm while cooking the remainder.

5 Arrange some of the Green Mango Salad on each dish, add 6 shrimp to each plate, garnished with coriander sprigs and serve immediately.

24 fresh large shrimp (1 1/2 lbs/700 g)
4 raw candlenuts or almonds
3 cloves garlic
3/4 in (2 cm) turmeric root, sliced
1 in (2.5 cm) fresh ginger root, sliced
1 egg, lightly beaten
1/2–3/4 cup (125–180 ml) water
1 cup (120 g) rice flour
1/3 cup (40 g) cornstarch
1/4 teaspoon ground white pepper
1/4 teaspoon ground coriander
2 teaspoons salt
3–4 kaffir lime leaves, sliced into fine threads
3/4 cup (115 g) dry-roasted peanuts, skins discarded, coarsely chopped in a blender
Oil, for deep-frying
1 portion Green Mango Salad (page 67), for serving
4 sprigs fresh coriander leaves (cilantro), to garnish

Serves 4
Preparation time: 25 mins
Cooking time: 10 mins

2 tablespoons oil
6–8 cloves garlic, minced
4 small shallots, minced
1–2 red finger-length chilies, deseeded and
    finely chopped
4 lbs (2 kg) fresh clams, washed and drained
2 dried sweet Chinese sausages (*lap cheong*),
    thinly sliced
1 can (14 oz/400 g) stewed tomatoes, blended
    to a purée
1 teaspoon coarsely ground black pepper
2 tablespoons chopped fresh coriander leaves
    (cilantro)
¼ cup (15 g) daikon or radish sprouts, to
    garnish
1 lime, quartered

Serves 4–6
Preparation time: 10 mins
Cooking time: 10 mins

Clams in red sauce with chinese sausages

This quickly made dish has an unusual fragrance and touch of sweetness, thanks to the rose wine used to make the dried sweet Chinese sausages. A mixture of garlic, shallots and chilies is briefly stir-fried, then the clams, sausages, tomato, black pepper and coriander leaves are added. Just stir until all the clams are opened, garnish with radish sprouts and serve with French bread to soak up the excellent sauce.

1 Heat the oil in a wok, then add the garlic, shallots and chili. Stir-fry over medium heat until softened, 2–3 minutes. Add the clams and sausages, increase the heat and stir-fry for 1 minute.

2 Add the tomato, pepper and coriander leaves and cook, stirring frequently, until the clams have all opened, removing each clam to a serving dish as it opens to prevent them from over-cooking. Discard any clams which have not opened, add the sauce to the serving dish and garnish with the daikon sprouts and lime wedges.

vegetable and tofu dishes

Crispy stuffed tofu with sweet chili sauce

Tofu is not only nutritious, but is remarkably versatile. In this recipe, it is sandwiched with layers of seasoned ground pork and crabmeat and then steamed. The cooked tofu is then dipped in flour and egg white and deep-fried for a meltingly smooth treat that is eaten with a sweet Thai chili sauce. Most of the preparation can be done in advance, making this ideal for entertaining.

$2/3$ cup (125 g) ground pork
Scant 1 cup (100 g) cooked crabmeat
$1/4$ teaspoon salt
Liberal pinch of ground white pepper
1 teaspoons minced garlic
4 small shallots, finely sliced
2 tablespoons chopped fresh coriander leaves
   (cilantro)
2 teaspoons oyster sauce
1 teaspoon sesame oil
1 teaspoon sugar
1 large cake firm tofu (10 oz/300 g), cut into
   4 flat slices horizontally, drained on paper
   towels
$1/2$ cup (75 g) all-purpose (plain) flour
4 egg whites, beaten until frothy but not stiff
Oil, for deep-frying
$1/2$ cup (125 ml) bottled Thai sweet chili sauce
1 teaspoon fresh lime juice

1 Process the pork, crabmeat, salt, pepper, garlic, half the shallots, half the coriander leaves, oyster sauce, sesame oil and sugar to a paste in a food processor. Place one slice of tofu on a heat-proof plate. Spread one-half of the mixture on this slice of tofu, then place a second slice of tofu on top. Do the same with the remaining tofu and filling. Arrange and press down gently with your hands to make even stacks.

2 Set the plate of stuffed tofu on a steamer rack over a wok of boiling water. Cover and steam over high heat, 15 minutes, then remove from the steamer, allow to cool, then chill in the refrigerator for 30 minutes. Do not refrigerate too long—just enough to cool down the outside but not the inside.

3 Cut each stuffed tofu sandwich into 4 cubes and coat each cube lightly with flour. Dip one cube into the egg white, turning carefully to coat all sides. Heat the oil in a wok until very hot. Deep-fry the stuffed tofu pieces until golden brown and crisp, about 2–3 minutes. Repeat with the remaining pieces of stuffed tofu.

4 Add the remaining chopped shallots and coriander to the Thai sweet chili sauce and lime juice and serve as a dipping sauce for the tofu.

Serves 4   Preparation time: 20 mins + refrigerating time   Cooking time: 20 mins

Sautéed mushrooms with dried chilies and cashews

This dish was inspired by a special type of Chinese mushroom known as *hou tou gu*—literally "monkey head mushroom" —due to its short spiky hair. If you are unable to locate these mushrooms in a Chinese grocery store, then use regular dried black Chinese mushrooms instead. A tangy sauce is added to the mushrooms after they have been blanched in ginger juice and stir-fried with chili, with a scattering of crunchy cashew nuts adding the final touch.

1 Wash the mushrooms and soak in warm water for 30 minutes to soften slightly. Squeeze out some of the liquid. Trim off the hard stems and cut into bite-sized pieces.

2 Process the ginger and water until the ginger is finely ground, adding a little more water if you are not able to obtain juicy young ginger. Pour the mixture into a sieve and press firmly with the back of a spoon to extract the ginger water. Bring the ginger water to a boil and blanch the mushrooms in this liquid for 1 minute. Remove the mushrooms, squeezing out some of the liquid, then briefly pan-fry them in a little oil over high heat to seal the moisture. Remove and drain on paper towels. Set aside.

3 To prepare the Sauce, combine all the ingredients in a small bowl, stirring until the sugar completely dissolves. Set aside.

4 Heat the oil in a wok and add the garlic, sliced ginger and dried chilies. Stir-fry over medium heat until the garlic turns golden, then add the mushrooms and green onions and stir-fry for 30 seconds. Add the Sauce and cook, stirring, for 1 minute. Add the cornstarch and stir until the Sauce thickens and clears, about 30 seconds.

5 Transfer to a serving dish and scatter the cashew nuts and sesame seeds on top. Garnish with the lemon rind and serve immediately.

6 oz (180 g) dried black Chinese mushrooms
4 in (10 cm) fresh ginger root, sliced
$\frac{1}{4}$–$\frac{1}{3}$ cup (60–80 ml) water
2 tablespoons oil
4 cloves garlic, thinly sliced
$\frac{3}{4}$ in (2 cm) fresh young ginger root, thinly sliced
2 dried red finger-length chilies, cut into short lengths, soaked to soften
1 green onion (scallion), cut into short lengths
2 teaspoons cornstarch
3 tablespoons lightly fried cashew nuts
1 teaspooon sesame seeds
Grated lemon rind, to garnish

SAUCE
$\frac{1}{2}$ cup (125 ml) chicken stock
2 tablespoons bottled sweet chili sauce
2 tablespoons Maggi seasoning or soy sauce
1 tablespoon black Chinese vinegar
1 tablespoon dark soy sauce
2 teaspoons oyster sauce
1 teaspoon sugar
1 teaspoon sesame oil
Pinch of Chinese five spice powder

Serves 4–5
Preparation time: 10 mins
Cooking time: 20 mins

1 carrot, diced
1 potato, diced
1 cup (150 g) sliced green beans
1 small zucchini, diced
¹/₂ cup (75 g) fresh or frozen green peas

SPICE PASTE
2 in (5 cm) fresh ginger root, sliced
3 cloves garlic
3 tablespoons oil
10 cardamom pods, slit and bruised
1 teaspoon brown mustard seeds
2 teaspoons cumin seeds
2 small onions, thinly sliced
12 curry leaves
1 teaspoon ground turmeric
1–2 teaspoons ground red pepper (cayenne)
2 teaspoons ground coriander
2 tablespoons water
2 tomatoes, diced
1³/₄ cups (400 ml) coconut milk
Additional salt, to taste

Simple vegetable curry

In this recipe, a combination of diced fresh vegetables (potatoes, carrots, peas, beans and zucchini) is blanched and then simmered in a delightfully spiced sauce of coconut milk and tomato. This vegetable dish would be ideal served with grilled fish or meat, although for a vegetarian meal, you could double the amounts and serve it with rice and a side-salad of cucumbers in yogurt.

1 To make the Spice Paste, pound or process the ginger and garlic together to make a paste, adding a little of the oil if necessary. Set aside. Heat the oil in a wok until very hot, then drop in the cardamom and mustard and cumin seeds. When the spices pop, add the onion and curry leaves, and stir-fry until the onion is light brown, 3–4 minutes. Add the ginger-garlic paste and stir-fry for 2 minutes. Add the ground turmeric, ground red pepper, ground coriander and continue to stir-fry until fragrant, about 2 minutes.

2 Add the tomatoes and cook uncovered, stirring several times, until very soft, about 5 minutes. Add the coconut milk gradually, scraping the bottom of the pan to dislodge any spices. Bring to a boil, stirring, then add the other vegetables and simmer uncovered until the vegetables are tender, about 10–12 minutes. Serve hot with steamed white rice.

Serves 4   Preparation time: 15 mins   Cooking time: 30 mins

Masala dosai rice flour pancakes

These delectable southern Indian rice flour sourdough pancakes are wrapped around a spiced potato filling and accompanied by a creamy yellow lentil dal, Tomato Chutney and Fresh Coconut Chutney (see pages 29 and 30). Prepare some or all of the accompaniments and the filling and batter the day before, then just quickly cook the pancakes and serve.

1½ cups (300 g) uncooked long-grain rice
¾ cup (150 g) black gram lentils
1 teaspoon salt
Oil, for frying
1 portion Tomato Chutney (page 29)
1 portion Fresh Coconut Chutney (page 30)

POTATO MASALA FILLING
1 tablespoon ground turmeric
2–3 teaspoons ground red pepper (cayenne)
2 tablespoons water
2 tablespoons oil
1 small onion, thinly sliced
1 teaspoon brown mustard seeds
10–12 curry leaves
4 potatoes, boiled and diced
1 teaspoon salt

YELLOW LENTIL DAL
2 tablespoons oil
1½ teaspoons brown mustard seeds
1 small onion, thinly sliced
2 cloves garlic, minced
10–12 curry leaves
1 dried red finger-length chili, cut into short
    lengths, soaked to soften
1½ cups (250 g) uncooked *arhal dal* (yellow
    lentils), soaked 15 minutes and drained
1 clove garlic, left whole
1 teaspoon salt
4 cups (1 liter) water
1 teaspoon ground turmeric
1 teaspoon ground red pepper (cayenne)
2 tablespoons water
1 small carrot, diced
1 small potato, diced
1 tomato, diced
1 red finger-length chili, sliced, to garnish
    (optional)
1 small onion, cut into rings, to garnish
1 sprig fresh coriander leaves (cilantro), to
    garnish

NOTE: To cook pancakes, it is important to have a thin batter and to cook over high heat. Do not flip the pancake until the top is completely dry.

1 To make the pancake batter, soak the uncooked rice and lentils overnight in a large pot of cold water. Drain and transfer the rice and lentils to a food processor. Process, adding a little water as needed until the mixture is very smooth. Transfer to a bowl, add the salt and stir in enough water to make a thin creamy batter. The batter should be allowed to ferment at warm room temperature for at least 4–6 hours or overnight, so that it becomes slightly sour.

2 Make the Potato Masala Filling by mixing the ground turmeric and red pepper with the water to make a paste. Heat the oil in a wok or wide saucepan and add the onion, mustard seeds and curry leaves. Stir-fry over low-medium heat, 1 minute, then add the spice paste and stir-fry for 2 minutes. Add the diced potato and stir to mix and thoroughly coat the potato with the spice mixture, 2 minutes.

3 To prepare the Yellow Lentil Dal, heat the oil in a saucepan and add the mustard seeds, onion, garlic, curry leaves and dried chili. Stir-fry over medium heat, 3 minutes. Add the drained yellow lentils, garlic, salt and water. Bring to a boil and simmer until the lentils begin to soften, about 15 minutes. Mix the ground turmeric and ground red pepper with 2 tablespoons of water to form a paste, then add this to the lentils together with the carrot, potato and tomato. Simmer until the vegetables are soft, 15–20 minutes. Garnish with the onion rings and coriander leaves.

4 Shortly before the pancakes are required, stir the batter and add more water, if needed, to achieve the consistency of a thin cream—the batter must not be too thick. Heat a large non-stick skillet and grease it with a little oil. Add about ⅓ cup (80 ml) of batter and quickly tilt the saucepan around to swirl the batter out from the center to the edges of the pan. Cook over high heat until the bottom of the pancake is golden brown and the top is dry, about 1½ minutes. Turn the pancake over and cook until golden brown on the underside, about 1 minute. Stack on a plate and continue cooking, to make more pancakes.

5 Fill each pancake with some of the Potato Masala Filling and serve accompanied by the Yellow Lentil Dal, Tomato Chutney and Fresh Coconut Chutney.

Serves 4   Preparation time: 20 mins + soaking time   Cooking time: 50 mins

Yellow Lentil Dal

Balinese mixed vegetables with crispy tempeh

Balinese-style mixed vegetables, Crispy Tempeh, Pickled Cucumber and Sweet Palm Sugar Sambal are commonly served as part of the composite dish Nasi Campur (Coconut Rice with Assorted Side Dishes), the recipe for which can be found on page 73.

2 cups (500 ml) water
1 teaspoon salt
2 cups (120 g) young pea sprouts (*dou miao*), or watercress
2 cups (120 g) spinach leaves
1 cup (150 g) sliced young green beans
1 cup (50 g) fresh bean sprouts
1/2 cup (50 g) freshly grated or moistened desiccated unsweetened coconut
1 red finger-length chili, deseeded and sliced
2 tablespoons Crispy Fried Garlic (page 31)
2 tablespoons Crispy Fried Shallots (page 31)
1/4 teaspoon salt
1/4 teaspoon ground black pepper
1/4 teaspoon dried shrimp paste (*belachan*), dry-roasted and crushed
1 tablespoon fresh lime juice
1 portion Sweet Palm Sugar Sambal (page 25), to serve
1 portion Pickled Cucumber (page 31), to serve
1 portion Coconut Rice (page 73)

DRESSING
2 tablespoons oil
2–3 cloves garlic, minced
1 tablespoon minced fresh ginger root
1 teaspoon ground turmeric
1–2 bird's-eye chilies, deseeded and sliced
1/4 teaspoon salt
1/4 teaspoon ground black pepper

CRISPY TEMPEH
1 teaspoon coriander seeds, lightly roasted
4 cloves garlic, minced
1–2 bird's-eye chilies, deseeded and sliced
1/2 teaspoon salt
2 tablespoons water
1 cake (5 oz/150 g) *tempeh*, diced
Oil, for deep-frying

1 Bring the water and salt to a boil in a saucepan. Add the pea sprouts or watercress and blanch for only 1 minute. Remove with a slotted spatula and plunge into cold water, drain and set aside. Do the same with the spinach leaves, squeezing firmly to remove excess water after cooling and draining. Blanch the beans for 2 minutes, drain and set aside. Blanch the bean sprouts for 10 seconds only, then chill and drain.

2 Place all the vegetables with the grated coconut, chili, Crispy Fried Garlic, Crispy Fried Shallots, salt and pepper in a bowl, tossing by hand to mix well. Refrigerate. Mix the dried shrimp paste with the lime juice, stirring to dissolve, then set aside until just before serving.

3 Make the Dressing by heating the oil in a small pan. Add all the ingredients except the salt and pepper and stir-fry over low-medium heat until fragrant, 3–4 minutes. Cool, then process to a paste together with the salt and pepper.

4 To make the Crispy Tempeh, dry-roast and then process the coriander seeds in a mortar or grinder until finely ground. Add the garlic, chilies, salt and process to a paste, adding a little of the water if needed. Transfer to a bowl, stir in the water, then mix in the diced *tempeh*. Set aside to marinate for 1 hour, stirring a couple of times. Heat the oil in a wok and deep-fry the *tempeh* over high heat until crisp and golden brown, about 2 minutes.

5 To serve, add the Dressing to the dried shrimp paste with lime juice mixture. Stir well, pour over the vegetable mix and toss well. Serve with the Coconut Rice, Crispy Tempeh, Sweet Palm Sugar Sambal and Pickled Cucumber.

Serves 4–6   Preparation time: 15 mins + marinating time   Cooking time: 20 mins

Tempura tofu salad

Combining the Japanese technique of tempura flash-frying with a Thai-inspired dressing, this quick and delicious dish makes a great starter or light meal.

1 Prepare the Sweet Chili Dressing by combining all the ingredients in a small bowl. Mix well.

2 Steam the asparagus spears until just cooked, about 3–5 minutes.

3 Put the tempura flour in a bowl and stir in the iced water, mixing with a pair of chopsticks. Do not over-mix; several small lumps are normal in tempura batter.

4 Heat the oil in a wok until very hot. Dip the tofu cubes in the batter, using two wooden spoons to turn and coat the tofu pieces well without breaking them. Carefully transfer the tofu cubes, one at a time, to the oil. Fry, turning to brown on all sides. Drain on paper towels and repeat with the remaining tofu and batter.

5 Divide the spinach, basil and asparagus into 4 serving bowls and add the fried tofu cubes on top. Drizzle with the Dressing and garnish with the Crispy Fried Garlic.

NOTE: If tempura flour (which gives the batter a very crisp light texture) is not available, use ³/₄ cup (100 g) sifted all-purpose (plain) flour and 1 egg yolk.

Serves 4   Preparation time: 10 mins   Cooking time: 15 mins

2 cakes firm tofu (10 oz/300 g per cake), cut into large cubes, then drained well and patted dry with paper towels
12 asparagus spears, thick ends trimmed
³/₄ cup (100 g) tempura flour (see note)
¹/₃ cup (80 ml) iced water
Oil, for deep-frying
2 cups (120 g) young spinach leaves, washed and drained
1 small bunch fresh basil leaves, plucked from their stems
Crispy Fried Garlic (page 31), to garnish

SWEET CHILI DRESSING
¹/₂ cup (125 ml) bottled Thai sweet chili sauce
¹/₄ cup (60 ml) fish sauce
¹/₄ cup (60 ml) rice vinegar
2 teaspoons sesame oil
2 cloves garlic, minced
1 green onion (scallion), minced

Vegetables in a mild coconut gravy

A favorite way of cooking vegetables in many tropical countries is to simmer them in coconut milk and spices. This is a simple recipe to prepare, using curry powder, garlic, shallots, ginger and lemongrass as the seasonings. Any sort of vegetables may be added and this makes a generous curry to serve with rice.

4 tablespoons curry powder
2 teaspoons ground turmeric
1/4 cup (60 ml) water
2 tablespoons oil
2–3 small shallots, finely chopped
4 cloves garlic, minced
1 tablespoon minced fresh ginger root
1 stalk lemongrass, tender inner part of
  bottom third only, finely chopped
3 cups (750 ml) canned coconut milk
1 cup (250 ml) water
1 teaspoon salt, or more, to taste
2 small onions, quartered
4 potatoes, cubed
2 carrots, sliced
1 cup (150 g) green beans, cut into lengths
1 Asian eggplant (about 5 oz/150 g), sliced
1–2 red finger-length chilies, left whole
8 broccoli or cauliflower florets
4 stalks okra, stems trimmed
2 tomatoes, sliced

1 Mix the curry powder, ground turmeric and water in a small bowl to make a paste.

2 Heat the oil in a large saucepan and add the shallots, garlic, ginger and lemongrass. Stir-fry over low-medium heat until fragrant and softened, 3–4 minutes. Add the curry powder paste and stir-fry for 2 minutes.

3 Add the coconut milk, water and salt. Bring to a boil, stirring frequently, then simmer uncovered for 2 minutes. Add the onions, potatoes and carrots, and simmer uncovered for 10 minutes. Add the remaining vegetables except the tomatoes and simmer for a further 10 minutes. Add the tomatoes and cook for another 5 minutes, or longer if needed until all the vegetables are tender. Serve with steamed white rice.

Serves 6–8
Preparation time: 10 mins
Cooking time: 40 mins

2 tablespoons oil
1 small onion, thinly sliced
1 small carrot, sliced into long, thin strips
1 small zucchini, sliced into long, thin strips
1 small Asian eggplant (about 5 oz/150 g),
    sliced into long, thin strips
1/2 bell pepper, sliced into long, thin strips
1–2 teaspoons curry powder
1 tablespoon plain yogurt
1/2 teaspoon salt
Ground black pepper, to taste
4 wholemeal chapati (see note below) or large
    soft tortillas
1 portion Pineapple Cucumber Raita (page
    30), to serve

CURRY SAUCE
6 small shallots
4 cloves garlic
1/2 in (12 mm) fresh ginger root
/2 in (12 mm) galangal root
1 teaspoon ground turmeric
2 candlenuts or macadamia nuts
11/2 tablespoon oil
1/2 teaspoon salt
2 kaffir lime leaves
1 teaspoon ground coriander
1 tablespoon curry powder
3/4 cup (180 ml) coconut milk

Note: You can buy fresh or frozen chapati or soft tortillas for this dish in most supermarkets. To make fresh chapati, sift 2 cups (230 g) wholemeal (*atta*) flour into a bowl with 1/2 teaspoon salt and 1 tablespoon clarified butter (ghee) or butter. Make a well in the center and add 2/3 cup (150 ml) water and 2 teaspoons oil. Mix well by hand to form a soft dough, knead for 10 minutes and rest 15 minutes. Divide into 6 portions, flatten each one in your palm by pressing with your finges. Roll one disc out into a thin pancake, 5 in (13 cm) in diameter. Cook on a dry, medium-hot skillet or griddle for 2 minutes. When bubbles start to appear, flip it over and cook until brown spots form underneath.

Serves 4   Preparation time: 10 mins
Cooking time: 25 mins

Chapati vegetable wrap

Wholemeal unleavened bread or chapati is normally dipped in curry gravy or lentils as part of a meal but in this creative recipe it's used as a wrap for a mixture of lightly stir-fried vegetables bathed in a fragrant coconut curry gravy. The fresh tang of Pineapple Cucumber Raita makes an ideal accompaniment.

1 To make the Curry Sauce, process the shallots, garlic, ginger, galangal, turmeric and candlenuts to a paste in a mortar or blender, adding a little of the oil if needed. Heat the oil in a small pan, add the ground mixture and stir-fry over low heat until fragrant, 3–4 minutes. Add all the remaining ingredients and bring to a boil, stirring. Simmer uncovered for 10 minutes, then discard the kaffir lime leaves. Set aside.

2 Heat the oil in a wok and add the onion, carrot, zucchini, eggplant and bell pepper. Stir-fry over medium-high heat until cooked but not soft, 2–3 minutes. Sprinkle the curry powder, then stir in the Curry Sauce. Remove from the heat and stir in the yogurt, salt and pepper. Set aside.

3 Reheat the chapati in a dry skillet or microwave, then transfer to a clean work surface. Arrange one-quarter of the vegetable and curry filling down the center of each chapati, then roll over to enclose the filling. Serve accompanied by the Pineapple Cucumber Raita.

Barbecued paneer and vegetables

This is an elegant vegetarian dish, normally cooked in a tandoor or clay oven. It uses firm Indian curd cheese or *paneer* (which is similar to baked ricotta), together with vegetables, marinating them in a chili-free or "white" tandoori marinade. Although it doesn't generate the same type of heat, an oven broiler works well for this dish.

8 oz (250 g) firm *paneer* (Indian curd cheese), or baked ricotta, cut into large cubes
1 green bell pepper, deseeded and cut into pieces
1 small onion, cut into wedges
1 tomato, cut into wedges
4 large skewers
Juice from 1 lime or lemon
Sprigs of fresh coriander leaves (cilantro), to garnish

WHITE TANDOORI MASALA
³/₄ in (2 cm) fresh ginger root, sliced
4–5 cloves garlic
1¹/₂ teaspoons fresh lime juice
1 tablespoon oil
2 teaspoons chickpea flour (*besan*)
¹/₂ cup (125 ml) thick natural yogurt
¹/₂ teaspoon *chat masala* (see note below)
¹/₄ teaspoon ground cumin
¹/₄ teaspoon mustard powder
Liberal sprinkling of ground white pepper

Note: *Chat masala* is a dried spice mixture consisting of *amchoor* (dried mango powder), cumin, black salt, coriander, ginger, salt, black pepper, asafoetida and capsicum. If it is not available, use normal curry powder and add more lime juice.

1 To make the White Tandoori Masala, process the ginger, garlic and lime juice to a paste. Heat the oil in a small saucepan and stir in the chickpea flour. Stir over low heat for 1–2 minutes to make a paste. Add the garlic and ginger paste and stir-fry for 30 seconds, then add all the other ingredients and cook over low heat for 1 minute. Cool before using.

2 Place the cheese cubes in a bowl then add half the White Tandoori Masala to the cheese and toss gently to coat. Put the bell pepper, onion and tomato in a separate bowl and toss with the remaining White Tandoori Masala. Refrigerate both for 1 hour.

3 Thread the cheese cubes, bell pepper, onion and tomato onto the skewers. Cook under a very hot oven broiler, turning several times, until done, about 5 minutes. Serve on the skewer or remove from the skewers and serve on a plate. Drizzle with lime juice, and serve garnished with coriander leaves.

Serves 4   Preparation time: 10 mins + refrigerating time   Cooking time: 10 mins

Tofu and vegetable salad with peanut dressing

This is a Singaporean and Malaysian hawker favorite, eaten at food stalls as a snack or appetizer. Firm cakes of tofu are deep-fried then tossed with a mixture of crisp bean sprouts, cucumber, carrot, pea shoots and lettuce, and topped with a spicy–sweet dressing made of crushed peanuts, dark soy sauce, palm sugar, chili, garlic and a touch of vinegar.

Oil, for deep-frying
1 cake (10 oz/300 g) firm tofu, dried with
  paper towels
2 cups (100 g) fresh bean sprouts, washed and
  drained
1/2 cup (50 g) cucumber matchsticks
1/2 cup (50 g) finely sliced carrot strips
1 red finger-length chili, deseeded and finely
  sliced
1/2 cup (40 g) green pea shoots (*dou miao*)
Several leaves soft lettuce, torn
1 green onion (scallion), cut into short lengths
2 tablespoons coarsely ground dry-roasted
  unsalted peanuts, to garnish

PEANUT DRESSING
1 red finger-length chili, deseeded
4 cloves garlic
2 tablespoons shaved palm sugar or dark
  brown sugar
4 teaspoons white vinegar
3 tablespoons dark soy sauce
1/2 cup (125 ml) water
2/3 cup (100 g) dry-roasted unsalted peanuts,
  skins removed

1 Prepare the Peanut Dressing by processing all the ingredients in a blender to make a thick sauce, then transfer to a large serving bowl. Set aside.

2 Heat the oil and deep-fry the tofu over high heat until crisp and golden on all sides, 3–4 minutes. Drain on paper towels, then cut the tofu into 1 1/4-in (3-cm) chunks.

3 Transfer the deep-fried tofu, bean sprouts, cucumber, carrot, chili, pea shoots and lettuce to individual serving plates and top each portion with green onion and ground peanuts. Serve with the bowl of Peanut Dressing so that each guest may drizzle the Dressing over the salad to suit his or her taste.

Note: Firm tofu may also be pan-fried with a little oil but the result will not be so crispy.

Serves 4   Preparation time: 10 mins   Cooking time: 8 mins

desserts
and drinks

Coconut cream custard

The rich, creamy taste of coconut permeates countless tropical dishes—from soups and curries to desserts. In this variation of the classic baked custard, coconut cream is combined with fresh dairy cream, sugar and egg yolks, with a dash of coconut liqueur adding even more fragrance to make a very special dessert.

2 cups (500 ml) fresh cream
¹/₂ cup (125 ml) thick coconut milk
¹/₄ cup (50 g) sugar
6 egg yolks
2 tablespoons coconut liqueur (such as Malibu)
4 teaspoons sugar
Fresh mint leaves, to garnish

NOTE: If you do not have coconut liqueur, you could add 2 tablespoons white rum and a few drops of coconut essence. For a lighter version of this recipe, substitute 1 cup (250 ml) of milk for 1 cup (250 ml) of the cream. Alternatively, use 1³/₄ cups (400 ml) milk and ³/₄ cup (180 ml) thick coconut milk.

1 Preheat the oven to 350°F (180°C). Place the cream and coconut milk in a saucepan and heat slowly, stirring constantly. Do not allow to come to a boil. Remove from the heat.

2 Beat the sugar and egg yolks together until the sugar is dissolved and the yolks frothy. Pour into the hot cream slowly, stirring constantly. Return the pan to the stove and cook over low heat, stirring constantly, for just 1 minute.

3 Strain the mixture into a bowl and stir in the coconut liqueur. Transfer the mixture to 4 individual heatproof bowls and set them in a baking dish of warm water. Bake in the preheated oven until the custards are set, 30–40 minutes. Cool the custards then sprinkle 1 teaspoon sugar on the top of each custard and brown under an oven broiler to form a caramel glaze. Garnish with a few fresh mint leaves, if desired.

Serves 4   Preparation time: 10 mins   Cooking time: 40 mins

2¹/₂ teaspoons gelatin powder
3 tablespoons hot water
8 oz (250 g) cream cheese
¹/₂ cup (125 g) superfine sugar
2 egg yolks
¹/₄ cup (60 ml) milk
1¹/₄ cups (310 ml) whipping cream, beaten

BASE
1 cup (2 sticks/250 g) softened butter
¹/₂ cup (100 g) confectioner's (icing) sugar
1 egg white
¹/₂ teaspoon vanilla essence
2 cups (300 g) all-purpose (plain) flour
¹/₂ cup (80 g) rolled oats

PASSIONFRUIT TOPPING
¹/₂ cup (125 ml) water
¹/₂ cup (125 ml) bottled passionfruit syrup or
   fresh passionfruit pulp
1 teaspoon gelatin powder
Sugar to taste

Serves 4
Preparation time: 10 mins + refrigerating time
Cooking time: 20 mins

Passionfruit cheesecake

Several varieties of passionfruit grow in the tropics, adding their wonderful perfume to a variety of dishes. This cheesecake, with a base containing rolled oats for a pleasantly firm texture, is covered by sweetened cream cheese enriched with egg yolk and combined with whipped cream and gelatin. When the cream cheese layer has chilled and set, it is topped with a glaze of passionfruit. This self-indulgent dessert provides plenty for second helpings.

1 To prepare the Base, beat the butter and sugar together until the sugar has dissolved. Stir in the egg white and vanilla essence, then fold in the flour and oats. Mix well, then press into a rectangular cake pan about 5 x 10 in (13 x 25 cm). Refrigerate for 30 minutes and, towards the end of the 30 minutes, preheat the oven to 340°F (170°C). Bake in the preheated oven for 20 minutes, until set and cooked, then remove and allow to cool.

2 Sprinkle the gelatin over the water and leave to soften and swell. Stir to mix well and set aside. Process the cream cheese and sugar to mix, then add the egg yolks, milk and gelatin mixture. Process until smooth. Transfer to a bowl and use a spatula to fold in the whipped cream. Spread evenly over the cooled base. Refrigerate until set, 2–3 hours.

3 When the cake is set, make the Passionfruit Topping. Combine all the ingredients in a small saucepan and bring to a boil, stirring. Simmer 1 minute, then transfer to a bowl to cool for 10 minutes; do not leave for any longer as it will start to set. Spoon the topping evenly over the cheesecake and return to the refrigerator for 10–15 minutes to set firmly.

Pineapple crumble

The popular apple crumble of temperate regions takes on a whole new meaning in the tropics when it's made with fresh pineapple flavored with rum and vanilla bean. Prepare the Crumble Topping in advance and refrigerate separately, then assemble and do the final cooking just before the meal for a trouble-free dessert.

1 small ripe pineapple (about 2 lbs/1 kg), peeled and quartered lengthwise, tough cores removed and reserved
1 tablespoon butter
4 tablespoons sugar
1 vanilla bean
1 tablespoon lemon juice
2 teaspoons dark rum
2 teaspoons pineapple liqueur, or additional 1 teaspoon rum
1 teaspoon cornstarch, mixed with 2 teaspoons water
1 portion Honey Yogurt Ice Cream (recipe below), for serving

CRUMBLE TOPPING
1¼ cup (185 g) all-purpose (plain) flour
⅓–½ cup (65–100 g) sugar (depends on the sweetness of the pineapple)
¼ teaspoon vanilla essence
½ vanilla bean, split
¼ cup (½ stick/60 g) chilled butter, diced

1 Preheat the oven to 350°F (180°C).

2 Dice the pineapple and reserve 2½ cups (500 g) of the diced flesh for the crumble. Process the remainder together with the cores to obtain juice.

3 Heat the butter in a large saucepan and add the reserved diced pineapple, 3 tablespoons of the sugar and the vanilla bean. Stir-fry over medium heat, about 5 minutes. Transfer to a bowl. Put ¼ cup (60 ml) of the pineapple juice, the remaining 1 tablespoon sugar, lemon juice, rum, pineapple liquer and cornstarch mixture in a small pan and cook over low heat, stirring constantly until the mixture thickens and clears. Add to the cooked pineapple, stirring to mix well.

4 To make the Crumble Topping, put the flour, sugar (according to the sweetness of the pineapple), both lots of vanilla and butter in a food processor and pulse until the mixture resembles breadcrumbs; do not over-mix. Transfer to a bowl.

5 Divide the pineapple mixture between 1 large or 4 small heatproof bowls, discarding the vanilla bean. Sprinkle the pineapple with the Crumble Topping and bake in the preheated oven until golden brown on top, 30–40 minutes. Serve warm with Honey Yogurt Ice Cream.

Serves 4   Preparation time: 15 mins   Cooking time: 50 mins

Honey yogurt ice cream

This delightfully fresh ice cream can be served with Pineapple Crumble or enjoyed with some almond biscotti or rolled coconut milk wafers known as "love letters."

¾ cup (180 ml) milk
¾ cup (180 ml) fresh cream
3 tablespoons honey
½ cup (100 g) superfine sugar
4 egg yolks
2 cups (500 ml) plain yogurt
1 teaspoon lemon juice

Serves 4
Preparation time: 5 mins + refrigerating time
Cooking time: 15 mins

1 Put the milk, cream and honey into a saucepan and bring slowly almost to boiling point, stirring constantly. Remove from the heat.

2 Beat the sugar and egg yolks together in a bowl until foamy, then slowly pour in a little of the milk mixture, stirring all the time. Combine with the milk mixture in the pan, return to the stove and cook over low heat, stirring constantly, until the mixture thickens slightly, about 3 minutes. Transfer to a bowl, cool, then refrigerate 30 minutes. Stir in the yogurt and lemon juice, then freeze in an ice cream maker. Transfer to a covered container and keep in the freezer until required.

3 Alternatively, if you don't have an ice cream maker, transfer the mixture to a metal cake pan, cover with aluminum foil and freeze until icy around the edges, about 1½ hours. Transfer to a food processor and blend to break up. Return the mixture to the pan, cover and freeze until firm, about 2 hours.

4 Transfer from the freezer to the refrigerator about 30 minutes before serving to soften slightly.

Tropical cinnamon fruitcake

The warm fragrance of cinnamon permeates this mixture of dried fruits, citrus juice and rind, flour, oats and honey. Make these in advance and store in an airtight container to serve any time a delicious snack is called for.

8 oz (250 g) dried mango, diced
12 oz (350 g) dried figs, diced
8 oz (250 g) dried dates, pitted and diced
1¼ cups (310 ml) oil
1 cup (250 ml) honey
½ cup (125 g) soft brown sugar
8 eggs
1 teaspoon vanilla essence
1 orange
1 lemon
1½ cups (185 g) all-purpose (plain) flour
1¾ cups (280 g) rolled oats
4 teaspoons baking powder
3 teaspoons ground cinnamon
2½ teaspoons baking soda
1½ teaspoons salt

1 Preheat the oven to 350°F (180°C).

2 Place the dried fruits in a bowl and add enough warm water to just cover the fruit. Soak for 5 minutes, then drain well, discarding the liquid.

3 Whisk the oil and honey together in a bowl, then add the sugar, eggs and vanilla essence. Grate the orange and lemon to obtain the rind, then squeeze to obtain the juice. Add the rind and juice to the bowl and whisk to combine.

4 Place the flour, oats, baking powder and ground cinnamon, baking soda and salt in a large bowl, stirring to mix well. Add the dried fruits and honey mixture, stirring to combine.

5 Transfer the mixture to a small greased non-stick loaf pan, pressing down firmly with the back of a spoon. Bake at 350°F (180°C) until set, about 30 minutes. Cool, turn out, then slice into bars. Refrigerate in a covered container for up to one month.

Serves 4
Preparation time: 15 mins
Cooking time: 30 mins

Tropical fruit smoothies

Delicious and healthy mixtures of soft tropical fruits, skim milk, yogurt, lime juice and honey make a great start to the day, and can also be enjoyed as a between-meal snack.

2 cups (500 ml) chilled skim milk
³/₄ cup (180 ml) chilled plain yogurt
1 ripe mango or guava, peeled, pitted and
    diced
1¹/₂ teaspoons fresh lime juice
4 tablespoons honey
4 ice cubes

Combine all the ingredients in a blender and process at high speed until smooth. Pour into four glasses and serve immediately.

Serves 4   Preparation time: 5 mins

Coconut palm sugar ice cream

This sinfully delicious ice cream is so satisfying that just a couple of scoops makes the perfect conclusion to any meal. Milk, cream and eggs are enriched with coconut milk and flavored with fragrant pandanus leaf and palm sugar.

1³/₄ cups (400 ml) milk
³/₄ cup (180 ml) cream
1 pandanus leaf, raked with a fork and tied in a knot, or a few drops pandanus essence
4 egg yolks
1 cup (250 ml) coconut milk
¹/₃ cup (60 g) shaved palm sugar or dark brown sugar
3–4 tablespoons dried shredded (desiccated) coconut, dry-roasted in a pan until golden brown, to garnish

1 Put the milk, cream and pandanus leaf into a saucepan and bring slowly almost to boiling point, stirring constantly. Remove from the heat and let stand for 15 minutes. Remove and discard the pandanus leaf.

2 Beat the egg yolks and coconut milk together in a bowl, then slowly pour in a little of the hot milk mixture, stirring all the time. Add this to the milk mixture in the pan and add the palm sugar. Cook over low heat, stirring constantly, until the mixture thickens slightly, about 3 minutes. Pour through a sieve into a bowl, cool, then refrigerate for 30 minutes. Freeze in an ice cream maker. Transfer to a covered container and keep in the freezer until required.

3 Alternatively, if you don't have an ice cream maker, transfer the mixture to a metal cake pan, cover with aluminum foil and freeze until icy around the edges, about 1¹/₂ hours. Transfer to a food processor and blend to break up. Return the mixture to the pan, cover and freeze until firm, about 2 hours. Transfer from the freezer to the refrigerator about 30 minutes before serving to soften slightly.

4 Garnish with the toasted shredded coconut.

Serves 4   Preparation time: 10 mins + refrigerating time   Cooking time: 15 mins

Banana chocolate surprise

This recipe could be seen as a variation on the popular mint-flavored chocolate. In this case, fresh mint and grated chocolate are mashed with banana, wrapped in a light pastry and deep-fried to make a most unusual dessert. You can prepare the pastry packets in advance and refrigerate them, doing the final brief deep-frying just before serving.

2 cups (300 g) all-purpose (plain) flour, plus extra for kneading
2 tablespoons oil
1/2 cup (125 ml) water
8 small strips pandanus leaf, to tie the packets
Oil, for deep-frying
4 tablespoons tropical fruit purée (mango, passionfruit, papaya or other fruits)

FILLING
3/4 cup (125 g) white or dark chocolate, grated
4 ripe bananas
1 tablespoon finely chopped mint leaves

1 Sift the flour into a mixing bowl. Make a well in the center and pour in the oil and water. Stir to incorporate the liquid, then knead the dough on a floured board for about 10 minutes until soft but not sticky, adding a little extra flour if needed. Divide the dough into 8 balls, then flatten each with your hand. Roll each disc of dough into a circle measuring about 5 1/2 in (14 cm) in diameter.

2 Prepare the Filling by mashing the chocolate, bananas and mint leaves together. (If working in a hot climate, put the Filling in the freezer for 5 minutes to chill the chocolate.) Put about 1 tablespoon of the Filling in the center of each circle and lift the edge of the dough circle to enclose the filling. Dab a little water on the inside of the neck area to help it stick and tie a small strip of pandanus leaf around the outside of the neck.

3 Heat the oil in a wok until medium hot. Deep-fry the samosa, a few at a time, until golden brown, 2–3 minutes. Drain on paper towels and serve hot or warm, with 1 tablespoon of fruit purée on each serving plate.

Serves 4   Preparation time: 25 mins
Cooking time: 10 mins

Soymilk pannacotta with tropical fruit

This lovely dessert uses milk made from soybeans, together with fresh milk and gelatin, to set it into a milky jelly. A garnish of tropical fruit balls adds color and freshness, while the fragrant pandanus-flavored sauce brings the tropics to the table.

1 First prepare the Pandanus Sauce. Put the milk and pandanus leaves in a saucepan and bring slowly to a boil, stirring frequently. Simmer, uncovered, 1 minute, then remove from the heat, cover and allow to infuse for 10 minutes.

2 Pour through a sieve, squeezing the pandanus leaves to obtain the maximum liquid and flavor. Discard the pandanus leaves.

3 Whisk the sugar and eggs yolks together in a small bowl, then pour in one-third of the infused milk, stirring constantly. Put this and the remaining milk back in the pan and cook over low-medium heat, stirring constantly, until the mixture thickens slightly and coats the back of a spoon. Cool, then transfer to a sauce pitcher.

4 Sprinkle the gelatin powder on ¼ cup (60 ml) of the soymilk and leave until it softens, about 5 minutes. Put the remaining soymilk and fresh milk in a saucepan and bring slowly to a boil, stirring. Add the gelatin mixture and sugar to taste (this will depend on whether the soymilk is sweetened). Return to a boil over low-medium heat, stirring constantly.

5 Pour into four 3-in (7.5-cm) hemispherical molds or glass bowls and allow to cool, then refrigerate for 1–2 hours to chill thoroughly. Unmold onto 4 serving plates. Arrange the fruit balls around each portion of pannacotta and serve with the pitcher of Pandanus Sauce.

Serves 4   Preparation time: 10 mins + refrigerating time   Cooking time: 10 mins

1 teaspoon gelatin powder
1⅓ cups (330 ml) plain soymilk
1 cup (250 ml) fresh milk
Superfine sugar to taste

FRUIT GARNISH
1 cup (125 g) fresh papaya balls
1 cup (125 g) fresh mango balls
1 cup (125 g) fresh dragon fruit balls

PANDANUS SAUCE
1½ cups (375 ml) fresh milk
3 pandanus leaves, raked with a fork, tied in a knot, or pandanus essence to taste
3 tablespoons superfine sugar
2 egg yolks

NOTE: If you cannot obtain pandanus leaves, prepare an equally delicious vanilla ginger sauce using 5 in (13 cm) sliced fresh ginger and a 3-in (7.5-cm) length of split vanilla bean in place of the pandanus leaves.

4 small tart pans or baking ramekins, each
    about 3 in (7.5 cm) in diameter and at least
    2 in (5 cm) high
1–2 teaspoons superfine sugar for sprinkling
    on the tart pans
³/₄ cup (85 g) finely ground almonds
¹/₃ cup (65 g) superfine sugar
2 large eggs
¹/₄ cup (35 g) all-purpose (plain) flour
¹/₃ teaspoon baking soda
¹/₄ cup (¹/₂ stick/60 g) butter, melted

TOPPING
1 tablespoon soft brown or raw sugar
1 tablespoon butter
4 thin slices fresh mango
4 thin wedges pineapple, or 2 small apricots,
    halved
4 thin slices papaya, or 2 ripe plums, halved
8 slices of banana, or 8 cherries, pitted
1–2 teaspoons superfine sugar

Note: To make one large upside-down fruit cake
for about 8 people, double the amounts of all the
ingredients and use a round cake pan 7 in (18
cm) in diameter with sides about 2 in (5 cm) tall.
Bake at 340°F (170°C) for about 35–40 minutes.

Serves 4
Preparation time: 10 mins
Cooking time: 35 mins

Upside-down tropical fruit cakes

Upside-down cakes are always delicious and especially so if the fruit used
is a luscious tropical fruit such as mango, pineapple, papaya and banana.
Other tropical fruits that would be perfect for this dish are guava,
pineapple and sapodilla (chiku). Even if you can obtain only temperate
climate fruits, you can still make this recipe, which has a rich almond
topping. Served warm with whipped cream, this impressive dessert is
ideal for a special occasion.

1 To prepare the Topping, put the brown sugar and butter in a saucepan and melt, stirring.
Add the fruit and sauté on all sides over medium heat, about 1¹/₂ minutes.

2 Grease the inside of the tart pans or ramekins. Sprinkle the greased part with 1–2 teaspoons
sugar, then divide the fruit evenly between the pans.

3 Put the almond, sugar and eggs in a food processor and mix at high speed until sponge-like.
Add the flour and baking soda, processing at low speed to mix, then pour in the melted butter.

4 Pour the cake mixture over the top of the fruit in each dish and bake at 350°F (180°C) until
done, 25–30 minutes. (A skewer inserted into the cake should come out dry.) Allow to cool
slightly, then unmold by running a knife around the inside of each dish and turning it upside-
down onto a serving plate, so the fruit is facing up. Serve warm with whipped cream.

Fried bananas with hazelnut filling

In this sophisticated version of the Balinese *pisang goreng*—bananas dipped in batter and deep-fried—you fill each banana with a sweet hazelnut-chocolate mixture before battering and frying it. You can use small finger bananas or regular large bananas.

1 cup (150 g) flour
3 tablespoons cornstarch
2 teaspoons superfine sugar
1 teaspoon baking soda
Pinch of salt
3/4–1 cup (185–250 ml) water
8 small finger bananas, or 4 regular bananas
Oil, for deep-frying

HAZELNUT FILLING
2 tablespoons shaved palm sugar or dark
   brown sugar
2 tablespoons water
1/3 cup (70 g) finely ground hazelnuts, dry-
   roasted in a skillet until golden brown
1 tablespoon cocoa powder
Scant 1/2 cup (50 g) confectioner's (icing) sugar
1 tablespoon lime or lemon juice

1 Prepare the Hazelnut Filling by heating the palm sugar and water in a small saucepan, stirring. Simmer for 2 minutes or until the volume is reduced to 2 tablespoons. Pour into a bowl and stir in all the other ingredients, mixing well. Set aside.

2 Put the flour, cornstarch, sugar, baking soda and salt into a bowl, stirring to mix well. Make a well in the center and stir in the water to make a thick batter. Set aside.

3 Peel each banana and make a deep lengthwise cut in each one. Spoon about 2 teaspoons of the Hazelnut Filling into the slit and gently squeeze the banana to close.

4 Heat the oil in a wok until very hot. Dip each banana in the batter to coat well, then carefully add to the oil. Deep-fry until the bananas are golden brown all over, 2–3 minutes. Drain well on paper towels and serve hot.

NOTE: You can save time by using a bottled hazelnut-chocolate paste such as Nutella, mixed with a little lime or lemon juice, to fill each banana rather than making your own filling.

Serves 4   Preparation time: 20 mins   Cooking time: 25 mins

Sweet black rice pudding with coconut cream

Served with Fried Bananas and a cup of strong black coffee, this black rice pudding is an indulgent way to start the day.

1 1/2 cups (300 g) uncooked black glutinous
   rice, washed and drained
1/2 cup (100 g) uncooked white glutinous rice,
   washed and drained
3/4 cup (180 ml) thick coconut milk

PALM SUGAR SYRUP
6 cups (1.4 liters) water
1/2 cup (100 g) sugar
2 tablespoons shaved palm sugar or dark
   brown sugar
1 pandanus leaf, raked with a fork and tied, or
   pandanus essence to taste
1 teaspoon salt

1 Put the washed and drained rice in a pan with enough water to cover by about 1 1/4 in (3 cm). Cook over medium heat and let the rice simmer until the grains are slightly soft.

2 In the meantime, make the Palm Sugar Syrup by putting all the ingredients in a large saucepan and bring to a boil, stirring until the sugar completely dissolves.

3 Add the Palm Sugar Syrup to the steamed rice and simmer, stirring from time to time, until the rice is very soft and the mixture has reached a porridge-like consistency, about 1 hour. Add more water if required to stop the rice from becoming too dry. Remove from the heat, discarding the pandanus leaf. To serve, spoon the pudding into individual serving bowls and top with the thick coconut milk.

Serves 4   Preparation time: 10 mins   Cooking time: 1 hour

Lassi iced yogurt drinks

Known in India as lassi, these deliciously refreshing iced yogurt drinks may be sweetened with sugar, lightly salted, or flavored with any fruits and spices of your choice. Our Spicy Lassi is blended with green finger-length chili; our Masala Lassi is flavored with a little onion, fresh ginger, curry leaves and fresh coriander leaves; and our Rose-flavored Lassi with Pistachios is an elegant combination that pleases both palate and eye.

Sweet lassi

2 cups (500 ml) chilled plain yogurt
1 cup (250 ml) chilled milk (or water)
2–3 tablespoons sugar
8–12 ice cubes

Put all the ingredients in a blender and process until smooth. Serve, or chill longer if desired.

Salted lassi

2 cups (500 ml) chilled plain yogurt
1 1/2 cups (375 ml) iced water
1/2–1 teaspoon salt
4 ice cubes
1/4–1/2 teaspoon ground cumin (optional)

Put the yogurt, water, salt and ice cubes in a blender and process until smooth. Serve with a pinch of ground cumin on top if desired.

Papaya lassi

2 cups (500 ml) chilled skim milk
3/4 cup (180 ml) chilled plain yogurt
2 cups (300 g) diced ripe papaya
1 1/2 teaspoons fresh lime juice
4 tablespoons honey
4 ice cubes

Combine all the ingredients in a blender and process at high speed until smooth. Pour into 4 glasses and serve immediately.

Spicy lassi

2 1/2 cups (625 ml) chilled plain yogurt
1/2 teaspoon salt
1–2 green finger-length chilies, deseeded and sliced
1/2 cup (125 ml) iced water
4–8 ice cubes

Put 1/2 cup (125 ml) of the yogurt, salt and chilies in a blender and process until smooth, adding a little more yogurt if necessary to keep the mixture turning. Pour through a fine sieve, pressing down gently with the back of a spoon. Discard any residue. Return the yogurt mixture to the blender, add the remaining yogurt, water and ice cubes and process for a few seconds. Divide between 4 glasses. Garnish with a few slices of chili if desired.

Rose-flavored lassi with pistachios

3 cups (750 ml) plain yogurt, chilled
3 tablespoons sugar
2 teaspoons rose water, or few drops rose essence
6–8 ice cubes
2 teaspoons finely crushed raw pistachio nuts

Process the yogurt, sugar, rose water and ice cubes in a blender until smooth. Transfer to 4 chilled glasses and sprinkle the top of each with 1/2 teaspoon crushed pistachio.

Masala lassi

2 1/2 cups (625 ml) chilled plain yogurt
1/2 teaspoon salt
2 tablespoons chopped fresh coriander leaves (cilantro)
10–12 curry leaves, sliced
1 tablespoon minced fresh ginger root
2 tablespoons finely sliced onion
8–12 ice cubes
1/4 teaspoon ground cumin

1 Put 1/2 cup (125 ml) of the yogurt, salt, coriander leaves and curry leaves, ginger and onion in a blender and process until smooth, adding a little more yogurt if necessary to keep the mixture turning. Pour through a fine sieve, pressing down gently with the back of a spoon. Discard any residue.

2 Return the yogurt mixture to the blender, add the remaining yogurt and ice cubes and process for a few seconds. Divide between 4 glasses and sprinkle the top of each serving with a little ground cumin. Serve immediately.

Serves 4
Preparation time: 5 mins

stockists

Most of the ingredients in this book can be found in large supermarkets or Asian food stores. Ingredients not found locally may be available from the mail-order purveyors listed below.

Australia
The Asian Sensation
www.ozebiz.com.au/asian

Germany
Asia-Laden
www.asia-laden.de

Elen's Asia Shop
www.asiatempel.de

India Food Company
www.india-food.de

Scandinavia
Siagians LM
www.asiatiskmat.virtualave.net/

UK
Bristol Sweet Mart
www.sweetmart.co.uk

Duan's Great Britain Thai Shop
www.flanakin.dial.pipex.com

Wing Yip Online Store
www.chinesestore.co.uk

USA
A Cook's Wares
www.cookswares.com

Asia Foods International, LLC
www.asiafoods.com

Bachri's Chili & Spice Gourmet
users.telerama.com/~bachris

Dean & DeLuca
www.deandeluca.com

ImportFood.com Thai Supermarket
www.importfood.com

IndoStores.com
www.indostores.com

Penzeys Spices
www.penzeys.com

SpiceEtc
www.spicesetc.com

The CMC Company
www.thecmccompany.com

The Oriental Pantry
www.orientalpantry.com

The Spice House
www.thespicehouse.com

acknowledgments

The recipes in this book were created by: **Four Seasons Resort Bali at Jimbaran Bay** Executive Chef Marc Miron **Four Seasons Resort Bali at Sayan** Resort Chef Vindex Valentino Tengker **Four Seasons Resort Maldives at Kuda Huraa** Executive Chef Frank Ruidavet **Four Seasons Hotel Singapore** Executive Chef Martin Awyong Chinese Executive Chef Jereme Leung

The publisher wishes to thank Neil Jacobs and the management and staff of Four Seasons Resorts and Hotels Asia Pacific for their generous assistance in the production of this book.

Special thanks to the following shops for the loan of their beautiful tableware and fabrics:

Club21
www.clubtwentyone.com

Galeri Esok Lusa
gundul@idola.net.id

Boutique at Four Seasons Resort Jimbaran Bay

PT. Jenggala Keramik Bali
www.jenggalashop.com

John Hardy
PO Box 2555 Tonja, Denpasar, Bali

Lotus Arts De Vivre
www.lotusartsdevivre.com

Narumi Serasi Indah
narumibl@indosat.net.id

Resort Shop at Four Seasons Resort Maldives

Sayan Shop at Four Seasons Resort Sayan

Props Credits
Page 2; 77 platter & napkin holder—Sayan Shop
Page 7; 76 chopsticks—John Hardy
Page 26; 32-33; 35 Jenggala Keramik
Page 27; 47 saucers—Jenggala Keramik
Page 28 shell & coral spoons—Lotus Arts De Vivre
Page 38 placemat—Resort Shop (Maldives)
Page 39 platter—Galeri Esok Lusa

Page 45 chopsticks—Jenggala Keramik
Page 48 shell & silver servers—Lotus Arts De Vivre
Page 50 plate—Jenggala Keramik
Page 51 platter—Jenggala Keramik
Page 55 coaster—Boutique (Jimbaran Bay)
Page 56 Jenggala Keramik
Page 57 silver bowl & shell spoon—Lotus Arts De Vivre
Page 59 placemat—Sayan Shop
Page 61 tray—Sayan Shop
Page 62 plate—Jenggala Keramik; mat—Sayan Shop
Page 64 bowl—Jenggala Keramik; cutlery—Boutique (Jimbaran Bay)
Page 67 silver & coconut plate—John Hardy
Page 73 platter—Narumi Serasi Indah
Page 81; 90 plates—Jenggala Keramik; tray—Sayan Shop
Page 84 plate—Jenggala Keramik; mat—Sayan Shop
Page 85 plate—Jenggala Keramik; tray—Sayan Shop
Page 88 chopsticks & fabric—Resort Shop (Maldives)
Page 89 plate—Narumi Serasi Indah
Page 93 platter—Jenggala Keramik
Page 102 fabric— Resort Shop

(Maldives)
Page 106 bowl—Jenggala Keramik; tray & basket—Sayan Shop
Page 107 cutlery—John Hardy; plate—Narumi Serasi Indah
Page 108 plate—Jenggala Keramik
Page 109 plate—Galeri Esok Lusa
Page 110 platter—Jenggala Keramik; lacquer dish—Sayan Shop
Page 116 horn bowl—Club21; gold fililgree chopsticks—Lotus Arts De Vivre
Page 124 silver & wood tray—John Hardy
Page 126 plate—Club21
Page 130 mat—Sayan Shop
Page 133 bowl & plate—Jenggala Keramik
Page 134 platter—John Hardy
Page 135 table setting—Jenggala Keramik; spoon—Boutique (Jimbaran Bay)
Page 141 bowl & plate—Jenggala Keramik

Thanks also to Mrs Ong Kiat Kim, Yaeko Masuda, and Magdalene Ong.